# Fresh!

# Fresh!

*An Introduction to Fresh Expressions of
Church and Pioneer Ministry*

David Goodhew
Andrew Roberts
Michael Volland

scm press

© David Goodhew, Andrew Roberts and Michael Volland 2012

Published in 2012 by SCM Press
Editorial office
13–17 Long Lane,
London, EC1A 9PN, UK

SCM Press is an imprint of Hymns Ancient & Modern Ltd
(a registered charity)
13A Hellesdon Park Road
Norwich NR6 5DR, UK

www.scmpress.co.uk

Scripture quotations are from the New Revised Standard Version of
the Bible, copyright 1989 by the Division of Christian Education of
the National Council of the Churches of Christ in the USA. Used by
permission. All rights reserved.

British Library Cataloguing in Publication data

A catalogue record for this book is available
from the British Library

978-0-334-04387-4
978-0-334-04459-8 (Kindle)

Typeset by Regent Typesetting, London
Printed and bound by
CPI Group, Croydon

# Contents

# Acknowledgements

The writing of *Fresh!* has taken place across several years. During this time we have received a great deal of help. We are grateful to Natalie Watson and the staff of SCM Press, both for suggesting the idea in the first place and for their encouragement and advice ever since. The staff and students of Cranmer Hall and the Wesley Study Centre in Durham, together with the participants of Fresh! – a course on fresh expressions based in York – have offered a hugely stimulating context in which to work on this book. Our thanks go to them for their support, insights and questions.

We are grateful to the staff of the national Fresh Expressions organization for all their help. A number of individuals have kindly read and commented on *Fresh!*, namely: John and Eileen Volland, Norman Ivison, Karen Carter and Ian Bell. Thank you to Lynda Barley and David Ison for information concerning Bradford Cathedral in Chapter 2. The Revd Gavin Tueno's doctoral research, 'Built on the Word: The Theology and Use of the Bible in Australian Anglican Fresh Expressions of Church', brought helpful insights from an Australian perspective. All the above have greatly helped the writing of this book; however, the responsibility for the views in this work is the authors' alone.

*Fresh!* is peppered with stories from individuals and individual churches. We are grateful to each person and each church for the insights and encouragements they have given us.

We are also grateful to the members of the fresh expressions and pioneer ministry research group, whose insights are quoted in Chapters 5–7: Jonny Baker, Ian Bell, Mark Berry, Mark Bryant, Steve Clarke, Jo Cox, John Drane, Ben Edson, Steve Hollinghurst,

## FRESH!

Chris Howson, Beth Keith, Joe Knight, Stephen Lindridge, Ellen Loudon, Ned Lunn, Ian Meredith, Chris Neal, Ben Norton, Dan Pierce, Janet Sutton Webb, Sue Wallace, Robert Warren, John Went and David Wilkinson.

We are conscious of all we have learnt from existing church communities that have nurtured, encouraged and challenged us – and been brave enough to begin new forms of Church. We wish to express our thanks to the people of St Oswald's, Fulford, York; FEIG in Gloucester and the Wolverhampton and Shrewsbury Methodist District.

Natalie Watson and Mary Matthews at SCM Press, Christopher Pipe and Neil Whyte have been helpful, efficient and encouraging – thank you!

Finally, we wish to express our deepest thanks, respectively, to Lindsey, Shona and Rachel, whose support, love and patience made the writing of this book possible.

David Goodhew, Andrew Roberts, Michael Volland
February 2012

# Introduction

# This Book is a Boat

*Fresh!* is a studyguide on fresh expressions[1] of Church and pioneer ministry. It explains why these practices matter and how to go about them, combining scholarly analysis with dozens of examples of fresh expressions and pioneer ministry in practice. *Fresh!* is designed like a boat, with three sections: rudder, hull and sails.

- The *rudder* consists of Chapters 1 and 2. In Chapter 1, scripture, Christian tradition and, pre-eminently, the doctrine of the Trinity, show us that God calls the Church to pioneer fresh expressions of Church. Chapter 2 looks hard at the experience of contemporary Britain, and finds many signs of hope for the Church to balance the more widely publicized signs of decline. These two chapters provide the essential theological 'steer' for fresh expressions and pioneer ministry.
- The *hull* consists of Chapters 3 and 4, which define what 'fresh expressions' are and the principles behind them. This is the 'body' of the boat, holding those who travel in it.
- The *sails* are Chapters 5, 6 and 7. Here are resources for individuals trying to hear God's call to pioneer new forms of Church – his call to grow more human in the process and to hear wisdom

---

1 In this book 'fresh expressions' (lower case) refers to concrete examples of new ways of being Church, while 'Fresh Expressions' (upper case) refers to the national team that supports this work. The Fresh Expressions team was formed in 2004 by the Archbishops of Canterbury and York and the Methodist Council to resource and enable the development of vibrant and sustainable fresh expressions of Church alongside traditional churches in parishes, circuits and deaneries across the country. The team has grown to include representatives of other denominations and mission agencies – see Chapter 3.

on how to go about this pioneering. The sails are necessarily flexible and fragile – in order to catch the wind of the Spirit.

David Goodhew built the rudder, Andrew Roberts took care of the hull and Michael Volland made the sails. Rudder, hull and sails are different from each other – and you will hear the individual author's voice in each part – but they are interdependent in function. If you intend travelling, we recommend that you pay attention to them all.

Being 'fresh' is part of Christian DNA. Thus the epitome of Anglican establishment, the Declaration of Assent, to which all Anglican clergy have to subscribe, contains these subversive words regarding the Church:

> It professes the faith uniquely revealed in the Holy Scriptures and set forth in the catholic creeds, which faith the Church is called upon to proclaim afresh in each generation.

'Proclaiming afresh' is, therefore, not some contemporary fad but is hardwired into church tradition. There has always been an urgency in the gospel message that will not permit us to wait for people to come to us – we have to go to them. We have to pioneer new ways of connecting with people if they are to connect with Jesus. We write this book from the shared conviction that doing Church in fresh ways, pioneering new ministries, is essential for all churches and all ministers in the current context – whether or not terms such as 'fresh expressions' or 'pioneer ministry' are deployed. This is not to paint a false division between 'contemporary' and 'traditional' – as this book shows, both are essential, both depend on and have much to learn from each other. Rather, it is to say that every priest, every minister has to facilitate the pioneering of new forms of Church – whether traditional or contemporary in form. Every parish, every circuit, every church needs to express Christian faith in a fresh way if it is to be truly a church. There is room for much freedom in how this is to be done, but the need for it to be done is, we believe, beyond question.

The need for fresh expressions and pioneer ministry does *not* mean jettisoning the immense riches of the Christian tradition. On the contrary, the best fresh expressions of Church will deeply value and be deeply rooted in historic practice and theology. But respecting the tradition is not the same as being traditional. Indeed, it is quite possible to be 'traditional' and yet misread the tradition. Faith rooted in the Trinity has always been a risk-taking enterprise, not a mandate for standing still. Specifically, any attempt at being fresh requires a far deeper engagement with the still neglected third person of the Trinity, the Holy Spirit. We argue that respect for Christian tradition will lead to a 'fresh' approach – and that it is excessive caution that fails to take seriously the historic inheritance of the Christian faith.

Who is *Fresh!* for? It is aimed at anyone training for church leadership, clergy and lay leaders and any Christian concerned to see the Christian Church effectively connect people with Jesus. David Goodhew and Michael Volland are Anglican clergy, while Andrew Roberts is a Methodist minister. Together we draw from our respective Anglican and Methodist traditions and from our experiences of starting new forms of Church, but each of us has learnt greatly from churches outside those communions and from the worldwide Christian Church. So *Fresh!* is written in a way that applies to a wide range of church contexts.

We have written *Fresh!* from the conviction that God has many new things he longs to do through his Church. We hope and pray that he may do much through you. And if this book aids you in that task, it will have more than fulfilled our hopes in writing it.

# I

# Fresh Expressions and Pioneer Ministry
# Central to the Christian Tradition

I handed on to you as of first importance what I in turn had received: that Christ died for our sins in accordance with the scriptures, and that he was buried, and that he was raised on the third day in accordance with the scriptures. (1 Cor. 15.3–4)

## Introduction: why bother with fresh expressions and pioneer ministry?

It may be that you are asking: 'Why bother with "fresh expressions" of the Christian Church? Why attempt to "pioneer" a new form of Christian ministry? Isn't the key thing to do the existing forms well?' Alternatively, it may be that you have been immersed in a new form of the Christian Church – and wonder why you should bother with more traditional forms, which you feel do not connect with the contemporary world.

Both these views have a point. In an age of fads and fashions, it's easy for churches to seek what's recent – 'froth expressions of Church' – as opposed to what's holy. Some scholars have attacked the theological basis of fresh expressions and pioneer ministry – with some justification. Conversely, some – *not* all – current forms of Church do not connect with the surrounding population, and a handful are close to death. Ignoring this fact is not showing 'faith'; it is being delusional. That raises the question of whether we need to go much further down the road towards fresh expressions and pioneer ministry than we have already. What then is to be done?

Making sense of fresh expressions and pioneer ministry requires a theological justification for these practices. This chapter provides that by offering three theological reasons why fresh expressions and pioneer ministry are central to the Christian faith:

1  They root us in the Apostolic Christianity of the New Testament, including the Christianity of Paul and the Corinthian church, to whom he wrote the words at the head of this chapter.
2  The Christian tradition, from the New Testament to the present, is about being fresh.
3  Because of who God is – the hallmark of God the Holy Trinity is that he is a God who pioneers fresh expressions of Church.

This chapter will unpack each of these statements of the Christian faith in turn. This leads into a further question: 'What does the contemporary context – the experience of living in the twenty-first century – demand of the Christian Church?' That will be discussed in Chapter 2.

## Apostolic Christianity

### The world of the early Church

In a post-*Da Vinci Code* world, it is widely assumed that the New Testament paints an inaccurate picture of historical reality. This is not a volume of New Testament studies, but we should emphasize here that we have good grounds to be sceptical of such scepticism! There is substantial and credible evidence to show the historical accuracy of the New Testament – as leading scholars such as Tom Wright and Richard Bauckham have shown.[1] Fergus Miller, not a biblical scholar but one of the foremost living historians of the ancient world, writes: 'The best introduction to this world is the Gospels and the Acts of the Apostles.'[2]

---

1 See, for example: N. T. Wright, *The New Testament and the People of God*, London: SPCK, 1992; R. Bauckham, *Jesus and the Eyewitnesses: The Gospels as Eyewitness Testimony*, Grand Rapids: Eerdmans, 2006.

2 F. Millar, *The Roman Empire and its Neighbours*, London: Duckworth, 1996, p. 195.

The ancient world was multicultural, multi-ethnic and had many different faiths. It was a mix of rich and poor, urban and rural. There was neighbourliness, freedom and culture, but much cruelty and warfare too. There were all kinds of gods and goddesses and all manner of philosophies, and people were free to choose between them as long as the overarching power of the state was acknowledged. It was a world in which key individuals and groups wielded huge power in politics, the military, business and culture. We could be talking of any Western society today, but all this was just as true of cities like the Rome and Corinth to whom Paul wrote the letters that form part of the New Testament. Even Jerusalem and Galilee were multicultural in a number of ways – Pontius Pilate had to write the sign over the crucified Jesus in three languages (John 19.20). It's easy to emphasize the differences between the world of the New Testament and our own, but we also need reminding of the many points of similarity.

The world of the New Testament was like ours in many ways, but harder and harsher overall. The narrow city streets were trodden by the wealthy in togas and by their slaves. Each lived in a world without modern medicine and with frequent epidemics, in which living beyond 40 was a notable achievement (Acts 4.22). Having children and being a young child in such a world was extremely risky and widows and orphans abounded. People were crammed together within the city walls in urban pressure-cookers that not infrequently exploded. The riot described in Acts 19 is recognized by historians as epitomizing the nature of life in an ancient city. No wonder people readily sought solace in a range of gods, goddesses and magical charms. The lid on the pressure-cooker was kept down by the Roman state and its army. The emperor in person might be far distant but he was forcefully present nevertheless – not least by often being declared 'divine' and therefore worthy of worship. But the lid was also kept in place by indirect means. From more benign forms such as the theatre, to the bloody safety-valve of gladiatorial shows, ancient society found a range of ways to live with its demons. This was a world in deep need of good news.

Conversion to the Jewish faith, while possible, was unusual. Moreover, stress on maintaining boundary markers between

Jewish and Gentile worlds discouraged traffic between them. Thus excavations of the temple mount in Jerusalem unearthed a stone inscription warning gentiles that if they came into the part of the temple reserved for Jews, they would be executed. By contrast, the pagan empire – in which most of the post-resurrection New Testament takes place – was on one level rather tolerant. There was a wide range of gods, and when Romans came across a new deity, that 'god' was simply added to the rest. In Bath, archaeologists have unearthed a temple to Sulis-Minerva. Minerva was the Roman god, Sulis a local British one – the Romans displayed a rough-hewn ecumenism by splicing the two together.

Being 'religious' in the empire meant offering sacrifices to whichever gods you were either obliged to sacrifice to or felt an affiliation towards. You didn't need to believe in them. The Roman poet Juvenal said of Roman religion, 'These things not even boys believe', yet participated enthusiastically in religious sacrifices.[3] Belief in these gods did not usually entail following a particular code of behaviour. Following Mithras or Isis had no more of an ethical dimension than, say, following astrology today. Ancient paganism had no notion of religious conversion in the sense of an exclusive change of faith and ethics. But while paganism had a degree of tolerance, this had tight limits. Every god was equal, but some were more equal than others. Notably, citizens were expected to offer sacrifices to the 'primary' gods, especially the emperor. You might not believe in them, but you had to worship them. Many of the early Christian martyrs fell foul of this dictum. So Roman pluralism might appear tolerant but was in practice intolerant. It absorbed the gods and goddesses of other cultures, but on Rome's terms.

With its wide range of nationalities and ideologies, the ideological context of New Testament faith has surprising resonances with our own context. They found themselves operating in this swirling mass of ideology, mostly with little wealth and little credibility. They faced many obstacles – laissez-faire paganism that couldn't see the point of deep conversion, and a Judaism so pro-

---

3 M. Green, *Evangelism in the Early Church*, Eastbourne: Kingsway, 2003, pp. 57–8.

tective of the God of the Old Testament that it was hard for others to draw close. In increasingly secular Britain we can identify more easily with the first Christians than has been possible for many generations. There are more than a few similarities between ancient paganism and contemporary relativism, which sees all forms of faith as equal and yet strictly adheres to a predetermined narrative.

In the ancient context, Christianity offered something very different. Unlike Judaism, it was passionately concerned to offer the good news of Jesus to everyone, Jew or gentile. Unlike paganism, the first Christians believed that accepting that good news meant an exclusive adherence to Jesus as *kyrios*, as Lord, and a growing conformity to the values of his kingdom – rather than seeing faith as an ideological supermarket in which you filled your trolley with whatever you chose (as long as you touched your forelock to Caesar). The early Christians made concerted efforts to encourage others to follow Christ. Acts shows Paul engaged for whole years at Corinth and Ephesus, arguing all day long with Jewish theologians (Acts 28.23), preaching through the night at Troas (Acts 20.11). He argued with passers-by in the marketplace of Athens, held extended debates in the lecture hall of Tyrannus in Ephesus and entered into extended dialogue with high-ranking officials like Felix and Agrippa.

The book of Acts presupposes the uniqueness of Christ and that encouraging people to follow Christ was both acceptable and essential practice within the Christian Church. Such presuppositions are problematic for many people in the contemporary West, which likes to see all faiths as leading equally to God. But rather than submit to the prevailing relativism, we need to test such a world view. Saying that all faiths lead to God sounds tolerant, but means boiling those faiths down to a common denominator, which has an uncanny habit of resembling modern Western thought. While speaking of the uniqueness of Christ can raise the accusation that the Church is being arrogant, that Church now operates in a post-Christendom context where, stripped of much of its power, it can speak humbly yet boldly of Christ.

## Why saying 'all faiths are the same' doesn't work

Saying that 'all faiths are the same' is a common view and can sound tolerant. But there are serious problems with this notion.

➤ It confuses the need to respect all people with the idea that you have to treat all viewpoints as equally true. Christians recognize, following Genesis 1, that everyone is made in the image of God and worthy of respect. But that doesn't mean each faith can be equally true. The different faiths differ markedly – so saying that they're 'really saying the same thing' means ignoring what each is *actually* saying, which is hardly showing them respect.

➤ Attempting to find a 'common denominator' between the faiths is difficult because it usually ends up looking like a version of modern Western thought – not a common denominator at all, just bolstering a specific viewpoint.

➤ Ignoring different views means ignoring reality. In important areas of life we recognize that we disagree. No one would suggest that Greenpeace and climate-change sceptics can both be right. To claim that contradictory opinions are really the same is to evade the issue over which they differ. To live is to choose.

➤ Classical culture helps us here. Roman society worked on the polytheistic principle that 'all faiths are legitimate – you just pick and choose'; only what was meant by this was that 'all faiths are available – as long as everyone doffs their cap to the emperor'. So too in our own day: saying 'all faiths are the same' requires us to doff our cap to the norms that govern modern Western states. Relativism as a creed is not tenable.[4]

---

4 For a detailed analysis of why seeking a common denominator between the faiths ends up with a variant of Western liberalism, see: G. D'Costa, *The Meeting of the Religions and the Trinity*, Edinburgh: T. & T. Clark, 2000. For an excellent analysis of how ancient polytheism and modern relativism are far from tolerant, see: C. Kavin Rowe, *World Upside Down: Reading Acts in the Graeco-Roman Age*, Oxford: Oxford University Press, 2009, pp. 159–72.

## Apostolic theology

The first Christians did two things: they bore witness to Jesus as Lord; and they formed a community. In theologian-speak, their Christology was an ecclesiology. 'Christian communities are the sociological explication of God's universal lordship in Jesus Christ.'[5]

The first Christians continually stressed that the historical Jesus was the lord, the *kyrios*. That had seven aspects:

1 Alongside the Old Testament they stressed that there was one God who had made the world and that the world was good. So while some parts of gentile culture were to be commended, others were to be rejected. Again, alongside the Old Testament they affirmed that human beings, Jew and gentile alike, were alienated from God, in large measure due to conscious decision on humanity's part, meaning that they (we) were living in darkness, living in an upside-down world.

2 Moving on from the Old Testament, they claimed that God had sent his Son, Jesus as Lord, to turn our upside-down world the right way up. The entire life of Jesus mattered, but the most important thing about his life was the way it ended – by execution on a cross, then resurrection from the dead. As a result everyone could know salvation, be 'saved'. This meant 'forgiveness of sins', but forgiveness of sins was not just about God accepting individual people, rather it was strongly corporate; it meant the restoring of outcasts as valued members of the community of believers.

3 Through Jesus, God had sent his Holy Spirit, so that the community who followed Jesus would have the strength to bear witness to Jesus.

4 The followers of Jesus were tasked with sharing the news of the lordship of Jesus with everyone, everywhere.

5 The main fruit of that witness was the establishment of communities of believers, which in turn bore further fruit by their witness in word and deed. These communities were formational

---

5 Rowe, *World Upside Down*, p. 126.

and countercultural – they destabilized the surrounding culture. But this destabilization did not take the form of challenging the state by insurrection – the early churches tried hard to be model citizens – but by the way they lived differently. Being Church was both theological and 'political' – but political differently from the way others were political.

6  The first Christians believed that the Jesus who had risen from the dead would one day bring an end to human history as we know it. They lived today in the light of Jesus' tomorrow – that was their 'eschatology'.

7  The first Christians offered a non-pluralist message in a pluralist age. They held the gospel to be as true for others as for themselves.

Thus the first Christians refused to see the good news as one option among many in the religious supermarket of the Roman empire. They would not keep the good news to themselves, as something that merely edified them privately – Acts contained a clear theory of mission, the good news of Jesus was for everywhere and everyone. The root prompt for mission was the cross and resurrection of Jesus. It was not a human programme for action, rather the only possible response to what Christians believed God had done in Jesus.[6]

But such witness was accompanied by deep listening to context. As Loveday Alexander shows in a study of Acts 10, the story starts with what God is doing in the gentile Cornelius' life. The job of the apostle Peter is to encounter Cornelius, to pray and to listen. This listening leads Peter to go beyond the threshold of Judaism, to discover that scriptures mean something other than what he thought they meant and that the power and plans of Jesus and the Holy Spirit were greater than he had ever realized.[7]

Such deep listening led to a continual process of translation visible in the New Testament. 'The kingdom of God', so promin-

---

6 These paragraphs are based primarily on Rowe, *World Upside Down*.

7 L. Alexander, 'What Patterns of church and mission are found in the Acts of the Apostles?', in S. Croft (ed.), *Mission-Shaped Questions: Defining Issues for Today's Church*, London: Church House Publishing, 2008.

ent in Matthew and Luke, was an expression rooted in Judaism and not easily translatable to gentiles, so as the Church spread into gentile communities, 'kingdom' tended to be replaced by the analogous notion of the lordship of Christ, which made much greater sense to that world (for example, Acts 11.20). Adoption was a gentile practice, rarely found among Jews – yet within a few decades adoption was central as a metaphor for the relationship of the believer to God (Rom. 8.14–17). Ultimately, every expression of Church in Acts was rooted in the Trinity and the scriptures and focused on the lordship of Christ. The first Christians were ready to allow the *context* of those they sought to engage with to shape significantly the *content* of their message – always recognizing that any enculturation of the gospel must not be at the expense of the countercultural nature of the gospel.[8]

The umbilical connection between theology and mission is illustrated by Acts, which sees the first Christian communities steadily moving out of their geographical, social, cultural and religious comfort zones in their effort to start fresh churches across the Roman empire. They started in Jerusalem and ended in Rome. Paul's letter to the Romans was written around AD 60, just 30 years after the death and resurrection of Jesus. He wrote to an already substantial and well-rooted Christian community nearly 1,000 miles from Jerusalem – one that had already been there for some time. When Paul and his companions stopped at different parts of the Roman empire, like Tyre in modern-day Lebanon or Puteoli in Italy, they found communities of believers there (Acts 21.3, 28.13), communities that, so far as we know, they had no hand in creating. The Christian gospel spread very widely, very quickly, often without official sanction from any leadership.

They began with Jews but irresistibly found themselves working with gentiles too. In one sense the entire book of Acts is the first fresh expression, with key specific moments of transition. The hinge between inherited and fresh expressions can be seen at the join between Acts 13 and 14. In 13, Paul and his companions

---

8 This last point is well made by Gavin Tueno, 'Built on the Word: The Theology and Use of the Bible in Australian Anglican Fresh Expressions of Church', DThM Proposal, University of Durham, 2011.

sought to start a church in a town called Antioch in the province of Pisidia (modern-day Turkey). Because their hearers were Jews, they rooted Christian faith in the words and practice of the Old Testament. They stressed the crucified and resurrected Christ, but did so through the lens they had inherited from the Jewish faith. Next they travelled to a place called Lystra. Here they were working with gentiles, people who were not ethnically Jewish, and their mode of operation changed totally. There were no references to the Old Testament, the book of God's *words*. Rather, Paul and his companions started with the created order, the book of God's *works*, pointing to this as a sign to the people of Lystra that there is a God. God, they said, 'has not left himself without a witness in doing good – giving you rains from heaven and fruitful seasons, and filling you with food and your hearts with joy' (Acts 14.17).

The early church communities, meeting mainly in houses, were necessarily small – dozens not hundreds of people. The first Christians were unembarrassed by this smallness, but there was a deep desire to grow. Hence Acts is structured as a geographical progression: Jerusalem, Palestine, Antioch, Asia Minor, Europe, Rome. And at each geographical transition the narrative contains summary verses, each of which speaks of growth (Acts 6.7; 9.31; 12.24; 16.5; 19.20). Growth was integral to the nature of the first-century Church. Christian theology was from the start missional.

## Apostolic praxis: an outgoing faith

Jesus preached and healed. Jesus gathered a team of followers whom he appointed as 'fishers for people'. Jesus initiated a new phase in the history of God's people by commissioning his followers to share his gospel – good news – with everyone: Jew and gentile, male and female, rich and poor. The good news was something you talked about and something you loved out; the message was word and deed. For the first Christians, the missionary message entailed a missionary praxis from the start.

Mission in the New Testament led to the foundation of ecclesial communities. Becoming a Christian was never just about an individual's faith in God: it meant joining a new family and learning a new way to live as a community, as believers together tried to grow more Christ-like. Thus Paul's letters are the letters of one deeply concerned that those outside the Church discover the love of Christ, but equally concerned that those inside the Church mature as Christians. Conversion and community were two sides of one coin.

The fresh expressions in the book of Acts were socially mongrel. A good number of the leaders may have been artisans, such as the fisherman Peter and the tentmaker Paul, but they found themselves in close fellowship with high officialdom and lowly slaves – for example, there was Lydia, dealer in luxury clothing (Acts 16.14). Yet Peter was to be found staying with a tanner – a profession held in contempt because the tanner 'stinks to high heaven'.[9] Many of the early Christians were slaves. They continually feature in Paul's letters, most notably in Philemon, which centres on Paul's attempt to reconcile a Christian slave with a fellow Christian, his master. Contrast Paul's letter to Philemon with this quotation from a papyrus written by an Egyptian slave owner:

> I commission you by this writ to go to the famous city of Alexandria and search for my slave about thirty-five years of age, whom you know. When you have found him, you shall place him in custody, with the authority to shut him up and whip him, and to lay a complaint before the proper authorities against any persons who have harboured him, with a demand for satisfaction.[10]

How meaningful for such a slave would have been the metaphor of *apolutrosis* – the technical term for freeing a slave – that the early Church used to describe Jesus' death, as the means by which the believer freed the slave from all guilt and offered eternal life.

The fresh expressions in Acts usually – not always – started with preaching, but didn't end there. Preaching was tied up with

---

9 P. Parsons, *City of the Sharp-Nosed Fish: Greek Papyri beneath the Egyptian Sand reveal a Long-Lost World*, London: Phoenix, 2007, p. 40.

10 Green, *Evangelism in the Early Church*, p. 169.

healing the sick and sharing with the poor. In Acts 2 the preaching comes first; in the next chapter it's the healing. Stories of healing and exorcism act as a counterpoint to ones of the founding of new churches. Within this community, healings and prophetic words were a key means by which witness to Jesus was made. This was to be seen both in the New Testament writings and, in the sub-apostolic era, in those of Justin Martyr and Irenaeus, for example. From a later period, the theologian Origen founded a school, but this combined didactic work with evangelism, prison visiting and manual labour.[11] Early Christianity was an experiential religion – you felt it as well as heard it.

And early churches were intimately communal. Early pioneers did make use of public halls, marketplaces and synagogues to engage with the local population. But with no public buildings of their own, churches necessarily gathered in people's houses. The household (*oikos*) was therefore 'the basic cell of the Christian movement'.[12] When we hear of how Christians 'broke bread at home', we should recognize that such homes were, for most people, small. Even the more affluent – and there were limited numbers of these in the early Church – would not have had room for more than a few dozen believers to gather. More often it would have been in small rooms – as in the third-floor room in a typical ancient low-rise tenement building in the city of Troas (modern-day Turkey), full of people, warm with the 'many lamps' lit so that they could meet during the night; so warm that it was easy to drop off to sleep when the preacher went on too long (Acts 20.7–9).

While the first expressions relied heavily upon the home, this was not home as we think of it. Homes in ancient cities were packed together. The sheer density of population made life far more public than it is today. Christian fellowship was close in every sense of the word. Central to that fellowship was care for those in need, within and beyond the fellowship. Supporting the needy and vulnerable was fundamental to being Church and made

---

11 Green, *Evangelism in the Early Church*, pp. 263–8, 313.
12 W. Meeks, *The First Urban Christians: The Social World of the Apostle Paul*, New Haven: Yale University Press, 1983, p. 75.

a great impression on the often divisive and cut-throat world of the ancient town.[13]

## Apostolic worship

The junction box between theology and community was worship. It was what you did 'when you come together' (1 Cor. 11.18). There are two mistakes that we can make in looking at the fresh expressions of worship generated by the early Christian communities: we can assume that because they were fresh they had no pattern, and we can assume that because they had a structure that structure was the same as the one we now use. So what *was* worship like?

Worship might include instruction, discussion, admonition, singing, prayer, thanksgiving, prophesying and ecstatic expression. Though there was order, it seems to have been a free order. However, there were two undergirding constants. First, worship was deeply scriptural. This was a Church that continually and deeply drank from the Old Testament, the Bible Jesus knew, and no less valued the 'apostles' teaching' (Acts 2.42), the teaching of those who had had closest contact with Jesus himself. Thus key writers of the churches that immediately followed the New Testament period – like Clement of Rome or Irenaeus – pepper their works with references to both the Old Testament and the apostles' teaching. Second, it was deeply sacramental, stressing continually baptism and communion. There was a deep concern that such actions were shared actions, so accounts of how Jesus first celebrated what we would call communion were treasured (1 Cor. 11.23–6). Communion had concrete social consequences. The forgiveness procured by Christ meant the end of social barriers – which were huge in a highly status-conscious society like the Roman empire. The sacraments were an apprenticeship into the spiritual life.

These actions took place not in dedicated buildings but in homes and – in the case of baptism – often in the open air. They

---

13 E. Ferguson, *Early Christians Speak: Faith and Life in the First Three Centuries*, 3rd edn, Abilene: Abilene Christian University Press 1999, pp. 205–13.

happened in a huge range of locations, across a wide geographical spread, among highly different groups of people. Strict uniformity was impossible, but the family likeness between these churches – rooted in scripture and sacraments – was unmistakable.

## Apostolic leadership

Apostolic leadership was inherently team-based, hence Paul's frequent reference to his fellow-workers. Considerable evidence exists of how senior church leaders stayed in contact with local leaders. Equally, the far-flung nature of the early churches and the limitations of ancient communications and transport meant that local leaders had a significant degree of autonomy. Churches might be started by one of the apostles, but local leaders swiftly had significant independence. However, it was not complete independence. Informal, relational control predominated, via a common ethos expressed in meetings, emissaries and letters. Given the low social standing of Christian leaders and the scattered nature of churches, informal control was all that was possible. Paul's letters vividly express the limited power of an apostle – for instance, where he is pleading with the wayward Corinthians – and the way that church leaders used written communication to cajole, command and encourage.

If oversight was loose, it was still real. The transport system of the Roman empire was as good as anything in Europe until the nineteenth century. Paul travelled around 10,000 miles in his work. Ancient culture was highly literate and the early churches took full advantage of this to forge connections between churches – hence so many of their early writings took the form of letters. Networking is not a new idea. Historians have pointed to the crucial role that apostles and bishops played in the growth of the Church in the decades following the New Testament. They provided continuity and oversight in a world of limited communications. Chapter 7 will look at the way coaching, mentoring and friendship sustain today's pioneer ministers. Similar processes can be seen operating in the letters of Paul and Peter and across the first centuries of the Church.

Pioneer ministry that focused on starting new forms of Church was thus central to the first Christian communities. We see in Acts how no sooner had the first church leaders set aside some members to oversee distribution of aid to poorer members of the community (the first deacons) than one of those so set aside was to be found sharing the good news, debating with the authorities and paying a high price for his actions (Acts 7). Amid renewed discussion of the nature of diaconal ministry, it is pertinent to note the role of deacons as evangelists. Central figures in the early Church found themselves responding instinctively to new situations in ways that significantly changed the way they did Church. Paul can reasonably be seen as a pioneer, constantly founding new Christian communities, appointing local leaders and moving on. Thus he wrote to the Christians in Rome of his desire to travel beyond them to Spain to start a fresh church in a place that had no knowledge of Jesus (Rom. 15.20). Many of the leading pioneers in the early Church combined that vocation with other ministries – as bishops, theologians or educators: Irenaeus, bishop of Lyon, 'was most at home as an evangelist'.[14] Pioneering was part of the DNA of the leadership of the early Church. The language of entrepreneurship can be used of pioneer ministry and will be explored in Chapter 5. It can be seen that many of the early Christian leaders could also be seen as religious entrepreneurs, ready to take risks for the sake of their apostolic mission.

What the New Testament Christians did not do is keep faith to themselves. Nor did they raise insuperable barriers to belief that would have meant, in effect, that only people like themselves stood any chance of getting in. The result was bound to be messy. Paul's letters to the new church in Corinth show that the Corinthians had some very strange ideas including that everyone was already resurrected. They had some seriously dubious practices worthy of a tabloid exposé. Paul did not anathematize them but sought to nurture this fresh expression of faith into Christian maturity.

The Christian faith has to root itself in the Christian scriptures and in the practices of baptism and communion as anchors of stability. But when we look at how the first Christians laid hold

---

14 Green, *Evangelism in the Early Church*, pp. 240–2, 300–17.

of the scriptures and the sacraments, we find that early Christianity was culturally highly adaptable. It had flexible mechanisms for control. It spread rapidly and untidily. It met most often as small groups in homes, a context in which uniformity would have been impossible. It was socially heterodox. It lived in a swirling sociological context; did not retreat from it but actively engaged with it. Apostolic Christianity was fresh.

## Apostolic: the key category for fresh expressions and pioneer ministry

The word apostolic, being 'like apostles', is hugely important for Christians. The Nicene Creed, central to all strands of Christianity, states that we believe in the 'only, holy, catholic and *apostolic* church'. Even Christians who are wary of traditionalism long to get back to the Church of the first Christians, which was led by the apostles. But there is confusion in how the term apostolic is understood. Clarifying what it means will help us see the point of fresh expressions.

Talk of apostles has tended to focus on *apostolic succession*, particularly via the institutions of the papacy and the episcopacy. While important, this has the effect of seeing apostolicity in terms of structures and authority. But apostolic can mean something else, namely acting in the manner of the apostles. This is something that touches all Christians. Seen this way, apostolicity is a kind of DNA that runs through the Christian community and appears in surprising ways – just as the Holy Spirit is likened to the wind: something powerful yet unseen and beyond human control (Acts 2.2).

'Apostle' means 'someone who has been sent'. Jesus is himself described as an apostle (Heb. 3.1). Those described as apostles in the New Testament are first and foremost the 12 who are sent out by Jesus. However, the term is widened to include other key leaders, notably Paul. There is some indication that women as well as men were apostles (Rom. 16.7). Apostles believed that they were sent, above all, to places where the Church was not.

Paul is the classic example – the restless leader who hoped to reach Rome so that he might continue to plant churches in Spain (Rom. 15.24), a destination he never reached.

The function of an apostle may usefully be summarized as a 'master-builder' (1 Cor. 3.10–15). Apostles built by founding churches and/or promoting their growth – both numerical and spiritual. They moved around a great deal – laid foundations but then usually left others to continue building. Yet they remained in touch with the churches they founded, praying for, encouraging and rebuking them. Apostles both witnessed to the good news about Jesus and embodied it by the web of relationships they facilitated. In the New Testament we see Paul both bearing witness about Jesus and, by the string of letters he wrote, expressing his concern to build up the community of Jesus' followers. Apostles were pioneers who sought to nurture fresh expressions of the Christian faith in places it did not yet exist.

A number of new churches in Britain have shown renewed attention to apostolic ministry for the Church of today, based especially on 1 Corinthians 12.28, where Paul places 'apostles' at the head of a list of ministries God has appointed for the health of the Church. Apostles are seen as having five characteristics:

1 Apostles were raised up by God as church planters.
2 The apostles' primary gift is to fit human relationships together so that congregations flourish spiritually.
3 Such leaders express authority primarily through personal relationships, have the right to appoint elders and often work in teams, which enables more to be done and junior team members to learn on the job.
4 Apostleship is reflected in geographical networks centred on individuals or small teams of leaders who have oversight of other leaders of largely autonomous churches.
5 There is a strong stress on the need to discern an individual's gifting, particularly though their work in a congregation.

This strain of thought holds that such apostolic ministry wasn't just needed in the first century but is essential for our own day.

And it's not a matter of using the term apostle but of acting in an apostolic manner. A strong stress on relationality is held to avoid the bureaucracy that has bedevilled existing denominations. Annual conferences, conventions or festivals are a key way of keeping networks together. This model has elements of both episcopal and presbyterian notions of church order but is distinct from both.[15]

New church theology and practice cannot simply be imported into other churches, nor is it without its difficulties. In particular, the attempt to read contemporary ecclesiastical practice straight off the New Testament does not recognize the impact of the intervening 20 centuries. Those centuries contain many groups that claimed an apostolic mandate but struggled to sustain their initial fire. More generally, the concentration of power in the hands of the 'apostle' requires safeguards. Nonetheless, new church thinking on apostolicity offers a challenge to mainline denominations as to whether they have defined 'apostolic' too much in terms of the apostolic succession and whether they (we) could learn by defining it rather in terms of acting in the manner of the apostles, whoever we are. What we see from the New Testament is that the apostles sought continually to start and nurture new churches.

Members of mainline denominations have sometimes been guilty of seeing the speck of sawdust in the eye of new churches and ignoring the plank in their own. In particular, new church understanding of apostolicity asks us:

- Is the apostolic function of starting new churches vigorously alive or sidelined in our denomination, locally or nationally?
- As we seek those to perform that function, are we testing such ministries primarily through the way they are evidenced in congregational life rather than other attributes?
- Do we prioritize relational gifts as the heart of the apostolic function, at whose core is the responsibility for ensuring that the relational glue within and between fellowships is strong?

---

15 W. Kay, *Apostolic Networks in Britain: New Ways of Being Church*, Milton Keynes: Paternoster, 2007, p. 246.

- Are we moving towards relationships rather than bureaucracy or inherited structures as the main visible connection between churches?

This view of being apostolic has much to say to episcope, the ministry of oversight exercised primarily by bishops in the Anglican, Catholic and Orthodox traditions – and Conference within the Methodist tradition or the General Assembly in the United Reformed Church. The notion of church planting has been largely alien to the Anglican episcopate and to bodies such as the Methodist Conference and United Reformed Church's General Assembly over the last 100 years. Their primary focus has been the maintenance of existing ministry rather than the founding of new churches. Rather than being centrally driven, church planting and new forms of church were grassroots initiatives in the 1970s and 1980s that then gained wider approval. By the creation and support for the fresh expressions movement, Anglican bishops and the Methodist Conference have belatedly begun to recover something of their apostolic function, but there is a long way to go. It could justly be argued that however much bishops and the Methodist Conference have claimed to be apostolic in terms of the apostolic succession, they often have not been apostolic in terms of emulating the passion of the apostles for starting new churches.

'Apostolic' has all too often been defined backwards, in terms of continuity – or supposed continuity – with the original apostles. But it can equally be defined forwards, as an expression of our 'sent-ness' by the Holy Spirit to awaken God's world to its true value in the sight of God. There is a deep need for this apostolic ministry.

## The Christian tradition

This forward-looking apostolicity is not only to be found in the early Church; it can be found across Christian history. Down the centuries, Christianity has a pattern of death and resurrection, a continual oscillation between decline and new life. The areas in which Trinitarian theology reached the height of insight and sophistication, what we now think of as Turkey, were the areas overrun by Islam. Many elements of Christian tradition which are thought of as deeply 'traditional' – for instance, an English prayer book, Methodism and the Franciscans – were at some point radical innovations. Truly, God is a God of surprises. There is something fresh in the heart of the Christian tradition.

Tradition is a tricky word. I was once in a church council where one member kept complaining that 'We at St John's feel . . .' and 'We at St John's want . . .'. Eventually one member of the church council, a very quietly spoken woman, turned to the speaker and said, 'I've been a member of St John's for many years, and you've never asked me what I think.' There was silence for a moment. It turned out that those who said 'We at St John's' actually represented no one but themselves. When any group of people assert that 'we' are this or that, it's always healthy to check what group 'we' represent – is it a widely based opinion or just that of a particular few?

We can treat the notion of Christian tradition in the same way – ascribing universality to something only a limited number of people value. But the Christian tradition is much larger and richer than that. It means the breadth of what has been accepted as Christian down the centuries and across the continents. That last qualification is especially important in the last century, as Christianity has spread across the globe and when Christian traditions outside of Western Europe are often far more vigorous than Christian traditions inside it. Christian tradition, moreover, is 'the democracy of the dead' in which we enfranchise those who lived before us and recognize that they have much to teach us.

The Christian centuries have been an epoch of continual, diverse, surprising mission. Innumerable examples could be cited – here are a few, selected to show the sheer breadth of the tradition of mission:

- The rise of monasticism: a reaction to the growing worldliness of Christianity as it became a more accepted part of society in the third and fourth centuries. Codified in the rule of Benedict, it became crucial to the spread of faith across Western Europe during the dark ages.

- The Christian faith spread beyond the Mediterranean through two monks, Cyril and Methodius, 'Apostles to the Slavs'. As ninth-century missionaries, they translated the scriptures and the Christian liturgy into the Slavonic vernacular, inventing an alphabet in the process – a work crucial to the Christian faith taking root across much of Eastern Europe.
- Saints Francis and Clare operated consciously and gladly within the mediaeval Italian Church, but by their radical espousal of poverty and service founded the Franciscan communities, which critiqued and regenerated much of mediaeval Christendom and have been a potent means for renewing faith for centuries.
- The Reformation can be seen as a string of religious innovations, operating across all traditions. The Anabaptists were arguably most radical in their attempts to found churches solely on a New Testament paradigm. Thomas Cranmer, while more of an 'establishment' figure, radically democratized English Christianity by translating the liturgy into the speech of the common people. Ignatius of Loyola was fervently Roman Catholic, and renewed existing forms of Church and led them into many new lands.
- The Evangelical revival saw diverse forms of theology from John Wesley, George Whitefield and Charles Simeon – Methodist, Calvinist and Anglican respectively. But they were united in their common work of starting new churches.
- The Oxford Movement consciously tried to be conservative in rooting itself in the thought of the early Church, but conservative roots bore radical fruit – especially through church planting and social compassion in the slums of booming Victorian towns.
- Pentecostalism, started by William Seymour in a Los Angeles storefront in 1906, was the most vigorous new form of Christianity in the twentieth century, with a massive, global impact, primarily among the non-white and non-Western world.

## Alexander Boddy

Alexander Boddy was an Anglican vicar of an industrial parish in Sunderland. Both priest and parish were obscure. Yet it was in this place that the greatest Christian movement of the twentieth century, Pentecostalism, first touched Britain. Boddy organized a series of 'Sunderland Conventions' in which the signs and wonders of Pentecostalism were experienced – in the setting of an Anglican church hall surrounded by steam-hammers and shipbuilding. Just as Pentecostalism started in a mixed-race storefront church in Los Angeles, so it landed in Britain in a place as far from traditional Christianity as could be imagined. Tracing British Pentecostalism's roots is an area of research in urgent need of work – but the long-standing work of Methodist pioneers in the North-East may well have produced seeds that, lying dormant for some years, were activated through Boddy's ministry.

This movement was already sparking across the world and is widely recognized as the most vibrant expression of Christianity in the last 100 years. The Pentecostal wine that Boddy experienced rapidly burst out of its Anglican wineskins and, for some years, appeared to be lost to that tradition. Boddy himself ended his days as vicar of the quiet rural parish of Pittington. However, from the early 1960s the charismatic movement re-grafted Boddy's insights into Anglicanism, and the resulting plant has borne great fruit. Boddy embodies the truth that, in the Christian tradition, splices fidelity to the past with innovation.[16]

It must not be thought that the extraordinary diversity of the Christian tradition implies that anything goes. Rather the tradition offers a polyphony in which multiple voices blend and old melodies can resurface sounding startlingly new. C. S. Lewis commented on studying the Christian tradition:

16 G. Wakefield, *Alexander Boddy: Pentecostal Anglican Pioneer*, London: Paternoster, 2007.

If any man is tempted to think . . . that 'Christianity' is a word of so many meanings that it means nothing at all, he can learn beyond all doubt, by stepping out of his own century, that this is not so. Measured against the ages 'mere Christianity' turns out to be no insipid interdenominational transparency, but something positive, self-consistent, and inexhaustible. I know it, indeed, to my cost. In the days when I still hated Christianity, I learned to recognize, like some all too familiar smell, that almost unvarying something which met me, now in Puritan Bunyan, now in Anglican Hooker, now in Thomist Dante.[17]

Christian tradition is often assumed to be primarily about continuity, yet that tradition is shot through with innovation. The backbone is provided by the scriptures, doctrines and historic praxis (most especially the two sacraments of baptism and communion), but this spine is part of a highly mobile body, shown in the fresh ways in which scriptures, doctrine and praxis are lived anew in each generation. It is therefore quite possible to be traditionalist in a way that betrays the Christian tradition – accepting only those static parts of the tradition and ignoring the tradition's incarnational spark that allows it to make Christ present in different generations and different localities; showing a nostalgic love of the form of faith while rejecting faith's radical content. Conversely, true 'fresh expressions' of Christian faith have a deep sense of their roots in the Christian tradition, blending the dynamism of the content of that tradition with an equally vigorous form.

Ironically, a church consisting solely of 'traditional' parishes falls short of the richness of the Christian tradition in a world where so many do not connect with 'traditional' Church. To be true to the Christian tradition requires entrepreneurial innovation. But a church consisting solely of fresh expressions also falls short of the Christian tradition in a world where many do still connect with inherited Church. Continuity and innovation are intertwined in the Christian tradition, and genuine expression of that tradition requires both. Humility tends to be thought of

---

17 C. S. Lewis, 'Introduction' to Athanasius, *On the Incarnation*, Crestwood, NY: St Vladimir's Press, 1996, p. 6.

in terms of individual discipleship, but there is a deep need for humility between the different strands of Christian tradition, to enable each to value the other.

## Holy Trinity: pioneering God

Christians believe that the God whom we meet in the scriptures and transmitted to us through the many strands of the Christian tradition is most truly described as the Holy Trinity – Father, Son and Holy Spirit.[18] God the Holy Trinity is to be worshipped rather than defined. Trinitarian doctrine is never an attempt to define God, which would plainly be futile. It is instead the mapping of God as he has revealed himself to us. But it is essential that we root our practice of Church in Trinitarian doctrine that best maps out what God is like. This section asserts the often ignored implication of Trinitarian thinking: that the three persons of the Trinity are pioneers. The Father, Son and Holy Spirit bring into being that which is fresh, not stale. Freshness is the hallmark of what they do. It could equally of course be said that God the Holy Trinity is a God of stability and order just as much as of innovation. The point being made here is that the innovatory nature of God is central to our understanding of who God is.

### Pioneering Father

Who is God the Father? The fatherhood of God is a neglected subject in our churches. Concerns over gender have helped mute focus on the fatherhood of God in recent decades. While understandable, it should be remembered that the early Church stressed that to describe God as 'Father' was not to ascribe gender to God – and the fatherhood of God is plainly central to the New Testament and to early Christianity in general. The early church thinker Augustine can help us here. He commented:

18 Renewed stress on the Trinity as the heart of Christian theology is one of the strongest shifts in Western theology in recent decades. See for instance C. Gunton, *The Promise of Trinitarian Theology*, Edinburgh: T. & T. Clark, 2004.

When God regrets something he is not changed, but he brings about a change. When he is angry he is not moved, but he does justice. When he is merciful he does not sorrow, but he sets free those who are sorrowing. And when he burns with love he is not aflame, but he inflames others.[19]

While not underestimating the issues raised by use of 'Father', use of alternative terms – especially impersonal names such as 'creator' – cause far greater problems by depersonalizing God. Tom Smail's *The Forgotten Father* points the way by suggesting that the Father is to be understood in three ways: as initiator, integrator and goal.[20]

Within the interrelations of the persons of the Trinity, the Father is the initiator. He is 'the fountain of the God-head, the source, cause or principle of origin for the other two persons'.[21] The Father is the source of all authority and lordship. The Son and the Spirit are equal in divine authority and lordship but they derive their powers from the Father. The Father exercises that authority and lordship by sharing it (John 14.28). Thus all three persons of the Trinity are involved in creation – yet it is the Father par excellence who is the creator of all things (1 Cor. 8.6).

God, by the creation of the cosmos, pioneers a new form of reality. Not content with things as they are, God begins something new. Not content with the relationships within the Trinity, God moves beyond them. God is love, and that love seeks new things to love, fresh ways to love. It is said that we learn of God through the book of his word (the Bible) and the book of his works (creation). It is immediately apparent that in so far as creation reveals something of God, God is keen on fresh forms of life. There is an ongoing debate about the precise number of species on earth – roughly eight million is the current estimate. But however many there are, the created order teems with new organisms, fresh expressions of life. And the same is true of people. A head-teacher at my children's school once said, 'I never get over the

19 B. Ramsey, *Beginning to Read the Fathers*, London: SCM Press, 1993, p. 51.
20 T. Smail, *The Forgotten Father*, London: Hodder & Stoughton, 1980.
21 K. Ware, *The Orthodox Way*, New York: St. Vladimir's Press, 1995, p. 32.

way that children raised in the same family, brought up exactly the same, turn out so different.' An examination of the 'book of God's works' points to a God who loves to innovate.

We mirror the initiating love of the Father by passing on what we have freely received. So Adam in the Garden of Eden is made assistant gardener, a co-worker with God in tending the creation. So Jesus gathers followers and entrusts to them the work of sharing the good news. All this comes from the Father who is at once the fountain of authority but exercises that authority in order to create. So if parts of our culture stand outside the culture of Christianity as it has been, we have to ask how we affirm the God-given aspects of that culture, those aspects on which God looks and sees that it is good – rather than ignore them or simply tell people to be like us. Just as Christians in Nairobi, Athens, Beijing and New York worship differently, just as Christians in the second, twelfth and nineteenth centuries worshipped differently, we need not be frightened of such diversity within our own churches. Belief in God as creator involves celebration of the diverse contexts of ministry and mission.

The Father is the integrator – within the Trinity and within the gospel. 'It is his purpose for his whole creation that gives meaning to the coming of the Son and the sending of the Spirit.'[22] To know the Father is to be recalled to the whole picture of salvation, where we see truly what is central and what is peripheral. This is a challenge to every part of the Church to hear what God is doing in those parts of it with which we are unfamiliar or even from which we recoil. If we are tempted to look down on more (or less) traditional forms of Church, let us remember the vastness of the body of Christ. Bearing in mind the centre of the gospel (the person and work of Jesus), how central are those differences?

The Father is the goal – of everything: the one to whom Christ 'hands over the kingdom' (1 Cor. 15.24); the one to whom Son and Spirit give glory. There is no autonomous 'realm of the Spirit' – it is entirely geared to showing us Jesus (John 16.15), and Jesus does nothing on his own authority, only what he sees the Father doing (John 5.19). Thus Jesus in the Gospels was not the slave

22 Smail, *Forgotten Father*, p. 16.

of the needs of those around him, rather his life was directed by his obedience to his heavenly Father. Jesus continually looked beyond the claims of human beings and was wholly focused on the claim of God.[23] So likewise, every expression of Church finds its goal not in being 'traditional' or 'fresh' but only in giving glory to God the Father and enjoying him forever. True worship – however traditional, however 'fresh' – is always far more than religious entertainment or mutual edification. It finds its goal as God-centred praise. Here is a challenge to every parish, every 'fresh expression'. The Church is not here primarily to meet our needs but to put us in right relationship with God as his adopted children – and this *does* meet all our needs.

## Pioneering Son

Jesus is the innovator: innovating by who he is (incarnation), by what he does (ministry) and by how he dies (cross) and rises again (resurrection). His message of the kingdom was clearly a shock to those around him. It fulfilled Old Testament hopes but in ways that surprised his hearers – it was fresh. The community he called into being didn't look as people expected it to look. The 'wrong' people kept getting in and the 'right' people faced hard questioning. That overturning of expectation was most acute in the final pages of the Gospels. The Christ, whose followers expected him to re-conquer Palestine, was executed by being nailed to a cross. And strangest of all, the Christ who was indisputably dead on Good Friday rose again on Easter Day.

The incarnation of Christ shows us that God is supremely interested in human beings – interested enough to become one of them if it means he can reconnect with them. Since they will not and cannot come to him, he goes to them. Jesus is God listening to humanity – by drawing near. He asks a Samaritan woman for a drink, knowing that Jews are not supposed to associate with Samaritans (John 4.7). He asks to stay with the rich fraudster Zacchaeus, knowing that would both affirm this small man and

---

23 Smail, *Forgotten Father*, p. 28.

force him to face his own duplicity. Christ's listening is not pas-
sive receiving of information but leads into God speaking words
of new creation – both literal words and the speaking that consisted of deeds of healing, exorcism and commands over nature.

The cross of Christ is God incarnate reaching out into that part
of human life most degraded: death itself. Humans cannot save
themselves. We cannot reach God, we cannot achieve peace with
others, we cannot achieve peace even within our own selves. We
are especially powerless against death. God in Jesus bears the
burden of human sinfulness on the cross: 'the son of man came
not to be served but to serve, and to give his life as a ransom
for many' (Mark 10.45). The image is clear: the price no human
effort could pay has been paid for us by Jesus on the cross. Jesus
refers to this on the night before he dies. Giving his followers a
cup of wine he says 'This is my blood of the covenant which is
poured out for many' (Mark 14.24). His death is the sacrifice that
leads to life.

This becomes clear after his resurrection. The resurrection of
Jesus meant the promise of restoration to life of our mortal bodies. Because human beings could not reach God, Jesus reconnects
us with God by his cross and resurrection. Jesus is the primal sacrament. Peter Oakes uses the findings of archaeology to create a
moving study of how the teaching of the apostle Paul would have
been heard in its original culture. In an ancient world of over-
crowded, often squalid cities – a world of deep social divisions
where poor health, natural disaster and social upheaval were
rarely far away the main message the mostly poor early Church
heard was the promise that by Jesus' resurrection they would live
beyond death. In a world where most faced great struggle, they
found in Christ that each was immensely valuable to God, too
valuable to be left to die.[24]

The incarnation, cross and resurrection are not all that Christians say about Jesus but they are the heart of it. They are God the
Son pioneering salvation for human beings. They are the starting
point of Christian mission. As Luke and Acts show us, mission

---

24 Peter Oakes, *Reading Romans in Pompeii: Paul's Letter at Ground Level*,
London: SPCK, 2009.

starts not as a good idea from the apostles but as their response to the action of God in raising Jesus from the dead. They did mission not because they wanted to but because they couldn't do anything else. The first Christians pioneered a new form of living because Jesus pioneered their salvation.

Jesus is the mission of God. Thus the Great Commission naturally comes at the end of Matthew's Gospel, as the culmination of Jesus' work: when who Jesus is (God's incarnate son) and what he has done (by the cross and resurrection) are plain, he charges his followers to spread the pioneering mission he has inaugurated – 'go therefore and make disciples of all nations' (Matt. 28.19).

## Pioneering Spirit

Freshness, we could say, is above all the hallmark of the Holy Spirit, the 'go-between God' (to use Bishop John V. Taylor's phrase). In Luke's Gospel the 'kingdom of God' is frequently mentioned. Yet in Luke's sequel, Acts, 'the kingdom of God' is little referred to. The focus is on Jesus as Lord, and the Holy Spirit is much more prominent, as the means by which people relate to Jesus. As has been remarked, the Acts of the Apostles could with justice be renamed the 'Acts of the Holy Spirit'. The Holy Spirit connects people with Jesus. It makes the Church happen. It is the gateway to the Father and the Son – thus 1 Corinthians centres on the cross and resurrection of Jesus – but these can only be appropriated by the Spirit (1 Cor. 2.12, 14). The Spirit is the means to the end, which is relationship with the Father through the Son. Thus the main names for the Spirit in scripture are wind, air and breath – things we see by their effects, not visible but utterly real. Since reaching out is the hallmark of the Spirit, any church that fails to emphasize the Spirit is likely to de-emphasize outreach.

Look at how the Holy Spirit operates across Acts. This is a book that begins with the ancient temple in Jerusalem and ends with a new church in Rome, hundreds of miles away on the other side of the Mediterranean. Along the way the first followers of Christ are scattered far and wide across the Roman empire. They meet a huge variety of cultures – from strict Jewish Pharisees to remote rural pagans to sophisticated Athenian philosophers. They try to incarnate the gospel in the diverse contexts and with the diverse peoples they meet. Luke sees all this within the umbrella of the Holy Spirit. It is the Holy Spirit above all that causes faith to arise and grow, enables the first Christians to form new expressions of Church beyond Jerusalem (Acts 1.8), is the rocket-fuel for Christian mission. The Holy Spirit envisions the first Christian believers (Acts 2.14–39) to share the good news of Jesus' death and resurrection with those around them. That same Spirit empowers them, gives them words to say, inspires their actions and inspires others to connect with God through those same words and actions. The Spirit who came from Jesus draws people to Jesus – here is a vitally important truth. The work of the Holy Spirit is the foundation for fresh expressions, pioneer ministry and church planting. Without the Holy Spirit they become an example of Christians working themselves into a pious lather for the sake of the gospel, and will always peter out. The Holy Spirit is God as Pioneer Minister – through whom all pioneer ministry finds its authentication and strength.

In a helpful image, Tom Smail likens the Holy Spirit to an artist whose subject is the Son but who is endlessly creative in the ways he depicts that subject.[25] The Holy Spirit operates in the same way as artists like Monet or Van Gogh, whose many pictures of haystacks or sunflowers are each subtly different. The Church is not endlessly pluriform for it is rooted in Christ. But it is endlessly inventive, because it is filled with God's breath – the Holy Spirit – who will not stay within the tramlines we set him. This makes sense of the huge variety of Christian churches both across the world now and across the past 20 centuries. They are related to each other but different.

In worship we are faithful to Christ by being rooted, pre-eminently in scripture and in the Upper Room. But good worship takes what happened then and translates it, gives faithful exegesis of it – through the breath of God's Spirit – into the very different circumstances of our 'now'. Ephesians 6.18 urges us to 'pray

25 T. Smail, *The Giving Gift: The Holy Spirit in Person*, London: Darton, Longman & Todd, 1994, p. 77.

in the Spirit on all occasions' – Christian worship only happens 'in the Spirit'. Worship is not just something we do for God but something God does *in* us. This liberates us from the stale debate as to whether 'traditional' or 'modern' worship is better. Neither is better. Worship that centres on 'what I get from it' misses the point of worship, whether it is ancient or modern. Any form of worship, if it centres on 'what I do for God', becomes mere technique. True worship starts with God and his Spirit: 'we do not know what we ought to pray for, but the Spirit himself intercedes for us with groans that words cannot express' (Rom. 8.26 NIV). All true expressions of worship are a gift from the Spirit.

The Spirit is the giver of fellowship – with God and with each other (2 Cor. 13.14; 1 John 1.3). The Spirit creates community. The Spirit is continually present even when we are unaware of it. We easily think of the Church as 'the body of Christ', forgetting that it is also 'the fellowship of the Holy Spirit' and can only become 'the body of Christ' through the work of the Holy Spirit. The Holy Spirit gives gifts through which the Church comes into being and is sustained. The Church is the sociology of the Spirit.

The Holy Spirit works in the coming of Jesus in his conception (Luke 1.35) and, in a similar way, he works in every Christian to regenerate our old humanity into a new humanity. The Spirit enables us to be born afresh (John 3.3, 5). Thus Richard Baxter, the seventeenth-century divine, wrote that 'to believe in the Holy Ghost is to take him for Christ's Agent or Advocate with our souls, and for our Guide, Sanctifier and Comforter, and not only to believe that he is the third Person in the Trinity'.[26] Every individual Christian needs that regeneration by the Spirit if their faith is to live – whether they belong to the most ancient of churches or the most recent fresh expression. 'He is not the Spirit of things as they are, of the status quo, but rather the Spirit of the future, the Spirit of things as they are to be when the purpose of God for his creation is complete.'[27] To be in the Spirit is to be alive, not to be

---

26 Alasdair Heron, *The Holy Spirit: The Holy Spirit in the Bible, the History of Christian Thought and Recent Theology*, Philadelphia: Westminster Press, 1983, p. 99.

27 Smail, *Giving Gift*, p. 168.

inert, to be capable of response to God (Gal. 4.6; 1 Cor. 12.3).
We could define sin as unresponsiveness – to God, to each other,
to creation. Life in the Spirit is to be purposeful, able to do God's
work (Acts 1.8). It is to be creative. The Spirit makes people creative portrayals of their risen Lord; the Spirit is the 'saint-maker'.[28]
Discipleship only happens by the Spirit.

The Holy Spirit works in Jesus at his baptism to enable him
to serve and save humanity (Luke 4.18–19). The Spirit anoints
Jesus to liberate others – and so too with us. The Church has a
specific mandate to ensure that the good news of Jesus connects
with those on the margins. The Church shares that ministry of
liberation – but such ministry is derived from and has authenticity
through being rooted in that same Spirit. It is striking how discussion on the gifts of the Spirit has focused on gifts such as healing and prophecy and not emphasized those gifts that lead to the
service of the poor and the liberation of the oppressed. Yet Paul's
lists of the Spirit's gifts include 'ministering . . . generosity (mentioned twice) . . . love . . . kindness' (Rom. 12.7–8; Gal. 5.22–23).
Social compassion is at the heart of the charismatic movement.

It is striking that Western Christianity, even now, continues to
downplay the Holy Spirit. Kallistos Ware, a bishop of the Orthodox Church, fairly critiques Western Christianity (Catholic *and*
Protestant):

> Inadequate attention is paid in western theology to the work of
> the Spirit, in the world, in the life of the Church and in the daily
> experience of each Christian. The living and immediate pres-
> ence of the Spirit has been too much forgotten, and so the Pope
> has come to be regarded as the vicar of an absent Christ, while
> the Church has come to be understood predominantly in terms
> of earthly power and jurisdiction and not in terms of divine
> grace and of a free and direct encounter with god in the Spirit.[29]

The most drastic illustration of this is the Eucharistic Prayer of
the communion service of the Anglican Book of Common Prayer

---

28 Smail, *Giving Gift*, p. 180.
29 Smail, *Giving Gift*, p. 134.

which, while excellent in many ways, comes perilously close to 'bi-nitarianism' rather than Trinitarianism in referring frequently to the Father and the Son, with scant reference to God as Holy Spirit. Contemporary liturgies have sought to correct this imbalance, but it takes more than liturgical revision to change the Western churches. Western Christianity's downplaying of the Holy Spirit has led to an overplaying of the role of the institutional Church, too scared of letting the Spirit blow where he will. The quickening of the Church in the contemporary West depends on a much deeper openness to the Holy Spirit.

This is not an issue of whether or not it is good to be 'charismatic', rather of a recovery of a fully Trinitarian faith. This is not about being in favour of or against 'fresh expressions' or pioneer ministry. But those who are wary of fresh expressions will only have credibility if they take seriously creative risks to connect those outside the Church with Christ. Powered by the Holy Spirit, that is how the first-century church acted. Much of what they did was in vain, but that did not stop them acting. A call to be fresh is in part a call to rebalance our doctrine of the Trinity so that the Spirit is no longer sidelined. Western Christianity still focuses too much on God as stable foundation and fails to do justice to the full range of biblical images of God that also speak of God as wind and fire. Western Christianity needs to freshen up. Jesus commanded his followers to do mission, not by commanding a particular missionary method, but by assuring them of his presence with them by the Holy Spirit (John 20.21–2)

## Pioneering Trinity

The Trinity is God the pioneer, God as missional. God the Father whose breath, whose Spirit, hovered over the waters, wanted something new, something fresh to come into being – and when it did, declared it to be 'good'. Jesus, God's Son, is sent out by the Holy Spirit after his baptism into the desert to pray and wrestle and then serve human beings. Jesus presses on, refusing the suggestion that he settle down. The disciples jog wearily behind him, unsure of his plans, complaining of what they have given up to

*Figure 1: Rublev's Trinity*

follow him, but he keeps going until he hits the cross – not that he stops there. God the Holy Spirit gushes out across the Mediterranean world, drawing the most unlikely people into an encounter with the risen Jesus, nurturing fresh communities of the most unexpected combinations – slaves and slave owners, Jews and Greeks, men and women.

The Father, Son and Holy Spirit bring into being that which is fresh, not stale. Freshness is the hallmark of what they do. The interplay of the three persons of the Trinity is for the purpose of mission. The Father sends the Son to the world; the Son reconciles the world to God; the Spirit makes the Son real to the world. But freshness, we could say, is above all the hallmark of the Holy Spirit.

Possibly the most widely used image for God as Trinity – Rublev's fifteenth-century Russian icon – depicts God in the form of three people around a table (Figure 1). The figures are so arranged that one side of the table is open to the person looking into the icon. It is as if the observer is being invited into the picture, invited to become the fourth member of the Trinitarian community of love. And because none of us is saved alone, that invitation means being part of a human community – a fresh expression of Church. Mark McIntosh, a leading modern theologian, describes the Church as 'an ever-fresh "event" continually coming into being as the human family is drawn into the pattern of Christ's relation to the Father'.[30] The fourth side of the table in Rublev's icon cannot be railed off. In the Christian doctrine of God, pioneering is at the heart of who God is.

### How do we define a church?

Here are some classic definitions:

- The Church is devoted to 'the apostles' teaching and fellowship, to the breaking of bread and the prayers' (Acts 2.42).
- The Church is 'one, holy, catholic and apostolic' (Nicene Creed).
- The Church is 'a congregation of faithful men, in which the pure Word of God is preached, and the Sacraments be duly ministered according to Christ's ordinance' (The 39 Articles).
- The Three Self Formula: a church is self-propagating, self governing, self-financing (Henry Venn, 1846).

---

30 M. McIntosh, *Divine Teaching: An Introduction to Christian Theology*, Oxford: Blackwell, 2008, p. 219.

- The Anglican 'Chicago–Lambeth Quadrilateral' sees the Church as constituted around four things: the Holy Scriptures, as containing all things necessary to salvation; the Creeds (specifically, the Apostles' and Nicene Creeds), as the sufficient statement of Christian faith; the Sacraments of Baptism and Holy Communion; the historic episcopate, locally adapted.
- Trinitarian, incarnational, transformational, concerned to make disciples, relational (Archbishops' Council: *Mission-Shaped Church*).

The traditional definitions are excellent in what they say but less helpful in what they leave out. Apart from Henry Venn's, none explicitly refer to the necessity of mission. It may be implied but it is not made explicit. The traditional definitions are Christendom definitions in which the population are assumed to be at least nominally Christian. *Mission-Shaped Church* remedies this in its definition of a 'fresh expression', but is detached from earlier definitions.

Moreover we live in a world in which Christian faith has faced serious critique, sometimes with good reason. The New Testament speaks continually of how all need to approach God with repentance and awareness of our shortcomings, and how all we do is founded on the freely given love – the grace – of God. This note needs adding to any definition.

So in a Western world that is largely 'post-Christendom', we suggest the following amendment of the traditional Prayer Book definition:

A Church is a congregation of faithful people, formed by the grace of God the Holy Trinity, in which the pure Word of God is preached, the Sacraments are duly administered according to Christ's ordinance and which is committed to joining in the mission of Jesus by word and deed.

## Conclusion

> I handed on to you as of first importance what I in turn had
> received: that Christ died for our sins in accordance with the
> scriptures, and that he was buried, and that he was raised on
> the third day in accordance with the scriptures. (1 Cor. 15.3–4)

The God of the scriptures, of the Christian tradition, the God who
is Father, Son and Holy Spirit, is a pioneering God. He reaches
out pre-eminently through Jesus (the pattern for all mission) but
Jesus sends his servants to express this tradition in fresh ways.
This mission of the exalted Jesus is accomplished by his followers
in the power of the Holy Spirit. As the Father sent Jesus, so Jesus
sends us through his Spirit. Christians are *apostolic* people, *sent*
people. What we are sent to do is to call people into God's new
society, which in turn transforms human society. We continue
God's mission but it is he who started it and who will complete
it. In the interval between now and the end of that mission, God's
people are resident aliens (to use a phrase from the theologian
Stanley Hauerwas). Our task is to be so rooted in Christ that our
lives point to the day when Christ will be all in all, and to point
those around us to Christ himself.

Why fresh expressions? Why pioneer ministry? Here are three
reasons:

- A Bible-based Church is necessarily a fresh Church, ready to
  pioneer new forms of Church. The book of Acts is in essence
  one long fresh expression.
- The Christian tradition is a long series of fresh expressions in
  which the central components of being Church are expressed in
  a kaleidoscope of churches translating the good news of Jesus
  into the huge variety of God's world.
- God the Holy Trinity shows that the essence of God is creating
  new forms of Church and longing to see the Church grow.

God in Christ reaches out to human beings wherever they are.
He comes to us. He does not wait for us to come to him. By seeking fresh expressions we reflect the love God expressed afresh in

his Son Jesus Christ, through whose pioneering Spirit he scatters communities following the risen Christ across the world.

Critics of fresh expressions are right to warn against 'froth expressions', which mirror a consumerist context in which novelty is the only fixed point. This is why all talk of fresh expressions, not least this book, needs to be rooted in a clear understanding of God as Trinity, rooted in the scriptures as the title deeds of the Christian faith, rooted in the sacraments as ancient fountains gushing life-giving water, and rooted the catholic Church as dependent, not independent.

But there is an opposite challenge to those whose form of Church has been inherited from the past. Many inherited forms are not nearly as securely rooted in the Christian God, the Christian scriptures and the Christian tradition as may be thought. Those who reverence tradition need to recognize the recent origins of much 'traditional' Church – and the ancient origins of some things that they question. Christian tradition goes back long before pews and cassocks and even before church buildings. Those who value scriptural preaching need to look hard at those scriptures – most especially the extraordinary book of Acts and its readiness to translate the Christian message so that it might be heard in the multi-ethnic world of the New Testament. Veneration for scripture can get in the way of modelling the evangelistic adaptability that the Christians of Acts showed. Those who treasure catholic worship, and especially the Eucharist, need to worry more about how the huge numbers of our fellow citizens who do not connect with existing forms of Church can be enabled to sit at table with our Lord and eat. Those who seek a radical faith need to espouse the radicalism of the New Testament, not a warmed-up radicalism of the twentieth century – a New Testament radicalism not willing to conform to the state-sponsored multiculturalism of the Roman empire, an empire that claimed to be inclusive and yet ran on its own distinct set of tramlines.

The key thing to understand about the Christian tradition is that it has always involved innovation alongside stability. The key thing to understand about new forms of Church is that the only innovations that last are those deeply rooted in the Christian tradition. The God whom Christians meet in Jesus and worship as the Holy Trinity is a pioneering God, reflected in churches that pioneer new communities of disciples, fresh expressions of the Christian Church. But the Holy Trinity is also the everlasting God whose purposes are constant and unchanging, reflected in churches of stable worship and love across the generations. Churches go off the rails through too much innovation or too much caution. The accent in this chapter has been on the danger of excessive caution. Looking around at churches in Britain, especially the mainline churches, it is difficult to argue that they suffer from an excess of innovation.

We live in a context closer to that of the early Church than that of the Christendom of the subsequent centuries; a world of many competing gods and much confusion; of profound needs and deep social divisions. We live in a world where the veneer of popular Christianity is now worn exceedingly thin or has disappeared entirely. In such a world we have greater appreciation of the purchase that apostolic Christianity had on its society – and can begin to appreciate that apostolic faith comes out of an apostolic God. God is inherently fresh. He calls into being that which is not. The Father sent his first apostle, Jesus, to share that life. Through Jesus the Father sends to us – as he has sent down the ages – his Holy Spirit to bring life to the people of God and through them life to the world. By the Holy Spirit we become apostolic in our Christian faith. Where might the Holy Spirit want to send you?

## Further reading

*Resources about the world of the early Christians*

Meeks, W., *The First Urban Christians: The Social World of the Apostle Paul*, New Haven: Yale University Press, 1983.

Millar, F., *The Roman Empire and its Neighbours*, London: Duckworth, 1996.

Oakes, P., *Reading Romans in Pompeii: Paul's Letter at Ground Level*, London: SPCK, 2009.

Parsons, P., *City of the Sharp-Nosed Fish: Greek Papyri beneath the Egyptian Sand Reveal a Long-Lost World*, London: Phoenix, 2007.

## Resources about the early Church

Alexander, L., 'What Patterns of Church and Mission are found in the Acts of the Apostles?', in S. Croft (ed.), *Mission-Shaped Questions: Defining Issues for Today's Church*, London: Church House Publishing, 2008.

Ferguson, E., *Early Christians Speak: Faith and Life in the First Three Centuries*, Third edition, Abilene: Abilene Christian University Press, 1999.

Green, M., *Evangelism in the Early Church*, Eastbourne: Kingsway, 2003.

Kavin Rowe, C., *World Upside Down: Reading Acts in the Graeco-Roman Age*, Oxford: Oxford University Press, 2009.

Stark, R., *The Rise of Christianity*, San Francisco: Harper, 1996.

## Resources about Christian theology

D'Costa, G., *The Meeting of the Religions and the Trinity*, Edinburgh: T. & T. Clark, 2000.

Heron, A., *The Holy Spirit: The Holy Spirit in the Bible, the History of Christian Thought and Recent Theology*, Philadelphia: Westminster Press, 1983.

Lewis, C. S., 'Introduction' to Athanasius, *On the Incarnation*, Crestwood, NY: St Vladimir's Press.

McIntosh, M., *Divine Teaching: An Introduction to Christian Theology*, Oxford: Blackwell, 2008.

Ramsey, B., *Beginning to Read the Fathers*, London: SCM Press, 1993.

Smail, T., *The Giving Gift: The Holy Spirit in Person*, London: Darton, Longman & Todd, 1994.

Smail, T., *The Forgotten Father*, London: Hodder & Stoughton, 1980.

Ware, K., *The Orthodox Way*, New York: St Vladimir's Press, 1995.

## Resources about contemporary mission

Archbishops' Council, *Mission-Shaped Church*, London: Church House Publishing, 2004.

Bosch, D., *Transforming Mission: Paradigm Shifts in Theology of Mission*, Maryknoll: Orbis Books, 1991.

Kay, W., *Apostolic Networks in Britain: New Ways of Being Church*, Milton Keynes: Paternoster, 2007.

Spencer, S., *The SCM Studyguide to Christian Mission*, London: SCM Press, 2007.

Wakefield, G., *Alexander Boddy: Pentecostal Anglican Pioneer*, London: Paternoster, 2007.

## 2

# Fresh Expressions and Pioneer Ministry For Such a Time as This

Thus says the Lord GOD: 'I am going to open your graves, and bring you up from your graves, O my people.' (Ezek. 37.12)

## Introduction: where are we?

The Christian tradition is a tradition of mission. How does that relate to such a time as this? How well fitted are the current practices of the Church to the present generation? Is this a world that has so changed that radical changes in church practice are needed – or is it a world in which tried and tested forms of Church are the best response? Chapter 1 asserted that the pioneering of fresh expressions of Church is central to the Christian tradition. This chapter, based on the latest academic research, will assert that such pioneering activity is central to addressing the context of contemporary Britain.

The contemporary Church in England has responded to its context broadly in one of two ways, encapsulated in two documents: the 2004 report of the Archbishops' Council, *Mission-Shaped Church*, and a widely read riposte, *For the Parish*, by Andrew Davison and Alison Milbank.[1] *Mission-Shaped Church* (MSC) has been the most prominent voice among a series of calls within the churches for creation of new forms of Church to connect with the large swathes of the population who show little or no inclination

---

1 Archbishops' Council, *Mission-Shaped Church*, London: Church House Publishing, 2004; A. Davison and A. Milbank, *For the Parish: A Critique of Fresh Expressions*, London: SCM Press, 2010.

to connect with the existing forms. The report recognizes the value of the latter but says that they are in themselves insufficient for the task of Christian mission. Andrew Davison and Alison Milbank, in *For the Parish*, have led the response that the 'traditional' parish is in robust health – and that stressing 'fresh expressions' is a mistake; that fresh expressions/church plants/pioneer ministry are, in significant measure, a harmful distraction from parish ministry. For such thinkers, it ain't broke, so we shouldn't fix it.

Explaining why churches grow or shrink is like bottling a sunbeam. There are no neat answers. The sociological and spiritual causes of growth and decline are multiple and complex. However, there is a large amount of good research, and while we cannot give a simple explanation, we can say a good deal. This chapter draws on a wide range of research on faith in contemporary Britain, much of it little known. It concludes that both MSC and *For the Parish* are partly right and partly wrong.

This chapter has two sections. First, it examines theoretical debates about secularization, showing that Christian churches need to face decline but should not be browbeaten by analysts who claim they are doomed. Second, it looks in detail at why some churches grow and others decline in contemporary society. While the notion of inexorable decline is wrong, we can learn a great deal from studying where British churches are growing and where they are declining.

---

## Comparing *Mission-Shaped Church* and *For the Parish*

*Mission-Shaped Church*

- Traditional forms of Church do not connect with large numbers – perhaps the bulk – of the population, so church planting and other new forms are needed.
- New forms of ministry are needed – beyond the traditional vicar.

---

- Secularization is a fact; many Christendom models of Church don't work.
- Draws on the history of church planting in the UK since the 1970s.
- Draws on experience of non-Western Church.
- Knowing what mission is tells us what the Church is.
- Form can vary, while content remains the same.
- Many different styles of Christian worship are valid.
- Anglicanism must learn from others, including newer denominations, independent churches and mission agencies.
- Fresh expressions.
- The Church should be Trinitarian, incarnational, transformational, concerned to make disciples, relational.

*For the Parish*

- The traditional parish system is what is needed.
- The main model of ministry is that of the traditional vicar.
- Don't overstress secularization; use Christendom models.
- Ignores church planting.
- Draws on experience of Western Church, especially in UK and America.
- Knowing what the Church is tells us what mission is.
- Form and content are inextricably linked.
- Traditional forms of worship, especially Anglo-Catholic forms, are best.
- Anglicanism is not one Church among many but is, in some measure, the true Church – although catholic and orthodox insights are important.
- Parish Mission Initiatives.
- The Church should be Trinitarian, incarnational, transformational, concerned to make disciples, relational.

Overall, both MSC and *For the Parish* have value, but also blindspots. MSC is right to point to the huge missionary task facing the Church and the need to innovate, but some of its theological underpinning needs work (such as loosely speaking of being 'incarnational' when what is meant is 'contextual'). *For the Parish* is right to celebrate the traditional parish and shows a considerable theological insight, but its theological edge is blunted by its highly idealized image of parish life, which fails to recognize the extent of secularization and ignores or rejects any Christian ministry that lies beyond a narrow definition of 'the traditional parish'.

## Secularization in contemporary Britain

Callum Brown wrote a highly influential study of British Christianity entitled *The Death of Christian Britain*. The battery of statistics and anecdotes Brown assembled have significant force – up to a point. There is substantial evidence that the mainline denominations have suffered deep decline in recent decades. There is debate about precisely when that decline began, but academic writers are clear that during the 1960s the curve of decline markedly steepened. There was a 50 per cent drop in Anglican Easter communicants during the twentieth century. Sunday School across the churches enrolment declined from around 50 per cent of the population to around 10 per cent during the century. The rate of baptisms per 1,000 live births declined from around 600 per 1,000 in 1900 to just over 200 in the year 2000.[2]

Brown's thesis is backed by other studies. Hugh McLeod shows that while in 1961, 94 per cent of Sheffield University students claimed a religious upbringing, in 1985 the figure was 51 per cent. A recent survey of Oxford University students suggests that over half see themselves as atheist/agnostic.[3] The 2011 census data

---

2 C. Brown, *The Death of Christian Britain*, London: Routledge, 2001.

3 H. McLeod, 'Being a Christian at the End of the Twentieth Century', in H. McLeod (ed.), *World Christianities c.1914–c.2000*, *Cambridge History of Christianity*, vol. IX, Cambridge: Cambridge University Press, 2006; S. Bullivant, 'Sociology and the Study of Atheism', *Journal of Contemporary Religion* 23.3, 2008.

about religion is still being analysed, but it indicates a further marked secularization during the last decade. Those who regard themselves as 'Christian' constitute 55 per cent of the population in 2011 – down from 72 per cent in 2001. Even more seriously, only 38 per cent of those aged 18 to 34 described themselves as Christian – for young adults in Britain, Christianity is now clearly a minority faith.[4]

Steve Bruce takes the evidence Brown offers and pushes it further. Brown sees secularization as specific to the experience of late-twentieth-century Britain. Bruce sees secularization as intrinsic to modern Western society as a whole. For Bruce, the churches in the modern West – and even God himself – are doomed. Bruce marshals a battery of statistics that convincingly show that most mainline denominations in Britain, taken overall, have been in serious decline for decades.[5] Thus it is clear that the United Reformed Church (URC), whose decline has been particularly severe, will shrink to a few thousand people by 2030 unless there is a profound change of direction. The Methodist Church has significantly shrunk in recent decades and is now much smaller than the Pentecostal churches, whom it dwarfed 30 years ago. The Anglican Church varies. In many areas it is declining just as steeply, but not in all. Anglican dioceses in the north of England declined between 1989 and 2009 by an average of 30 per cent. The best-performing diocese declined by just under 20 per cent, the worst by almost 40 per cent. However, some Anglican dioceses are declining by a much smaller amount and one, London, has seen sustained growth over this period.[6]

---

4 www.yougov.polis.cam.ac.uk/archive, accessed 21 September 2011.

5 S. Bruce, *God is Dead: Secularization in the West*, Oxford: Blackwell, 2002.

6 Figures taken from B. Jackson, *Hope for the Church*, London: Church House Publishing, 2002; B. Jackson, 'Hope for the North?', paper given at 'Church:North' conference, 25 February 2011, Cranmer Hall, Durham; B. Jackson and J. Wolffe, 'Anglican Resurgence: The Church of England in London', in D. Goodhew (ed.), *Church Growth in Britain from 1980 to the Present Day*, Farnham: Ashgate, 2012.

## Mainline Sunday church attendance[7]

|          | 1990      | 2000      | 2010    |
|----------|-----------|-----------|---------|
| RC       | 1,571,000 | 1,090,400 | 736,600 |
| CofE     | 1,259,800 | 963,300   | 780,000 |
| Methodist| 506,400   | 372,600   | 248,800 |
| URC      | 141,500   | 112,000   | 55,700  |

Secularization has occurred in the form of the shrinkage of some churches and the loss of belief by some individuals, but also on a societal level. The secularity of most TV and radio programmes, the marginalization of faith in much state schooling and the conversion of Sunday into a day of shopping are examples of the ways in which Christian faith – and sometimes faith in general – is increasingly pushed to the margins. Other scholars, notably Grace Davie, have pointed to how Christian faith retains a significant purchase on British society, but the trend is clear.

Brown and Bruce make untenable the notion that the traditional church and the traditional parish system remain in rude health. This is a serious problem for Davison's and Milbank's *For the Parish*. Their critique of fresh expressions has some force but makes no reference to the widespread decline of many traditional parishes, nor the disconnection between much of society and Christian faith. It is noticeable how many of the examples of good practice in *For the Parish* are drawn not from parishes but from cathedrals and Oxbridge college chapels, forms of Church at one remove from the realities facing most local churches and insulated, in part, from the chill winds of secularity by inherited resources and class structure. The period of history with which *For the Parish* most frequently quarries for examples is the middle ages – a period whose unquestioning acceptance of Christendom stands in stark variance with the culture of contemporary Britain.[8]

---

7 P. Brierley (ed.), *Religious Trends 7, 2007–8: British Religion in the Twenty-First Century*, Swindon: Christian Research, 2008, 2.24.

8 Davison and Milbank, *For the Parish*, pp. 82–3, 146–50, 186, 192, 197, 203, 207.

## Does all this Talk of Numbers Matter?

All these statistics – how important are they? Is concern about numbers neurotic or, worse, an ungodly obsession with 'bigging ourselves up'?

This is a thought in many minds. Here are some common questions raised about bothering with 'bums on seats', along with some answers.

*Isn't it the case that the kingdom of God matters, not the Church?*

Yes, Jesus said a lot about the kingdom of God but he didn't play it off against the Church. The New Testament sees the Church as a kind of base camp for the kingdom. Jesus loved and cared for the small group of disciples who closely followed him, and cared for and loved the wider society. So we shouldn't play kingdom and Church off against each other. We need both.

*Isn't quality more important than quantity when it comes to the size of a church?*

- Yes, of course, the quality of a church matters more than its size. But as we saw in the last chapter, growing the community of believers was central to Jesus' mission.
- Moreover, falling numbers in an organization is often a sign that the quality of that organization is declining and/or that it has lost touch with the wider society – we should be concerned to rectify the shrinking size of many churches *and* improve the quality of what we do.
- Quantity and quality go together. Quantitative church growth generally reflects qualitative church growth. It's not 'either–or'.

*Isn't small often beautiful ?*

Large communities of Christians can be bland or even corrupt, their faith 'a mile wide and an inch deep'. But just to say that is a fatalistic attitude – larger groups can also do more good than smaller ones. Many churches have backed the Fair Trade movement, and the size of that support is a major reason Fair Trade has become much more significant as a means of lifting people out of poverty. To a degree, size is significant.

*Isn't the church there primarily for others – so getting concerned about our growth/decline is irrelevant?*

- Yes, central to the life of the Church is its care for those who don't belong to it; care for every member of the community, for the Third World, care for the sick, the poor and the marginalized in this country.
- But that care will be far less effective if it is done by a dwindling, ageing group of people, than if it is done by a growing, all-age community.
- Moreover, when we stress 'care for others', we often exclude caring for them by seeking to introduce them to the eternal love of God in Jesus – which is central to how we can best care for them.

*Isn't it intolerant to try to encourage others to follow Jesus?*

- This widespread concern was covered in the previous chapter. Intolerance is wrong, but so is indifference. It is right and good to share faith, if we do so in a caring manner.
- The New Testament shows Christians and churches doing all they can to encourage others to follow Jesus, but doing so by sharing good news in a loving way – 'with gentleness and reverence' (1 Peter 3.15).

More positively, here are reasons why numbers should matter to us and, more importantly, do matter to God:

- Jesus and his first followers strove to share the good news of forgiveness from God and the hope of God with as many people as they could – if we aim to follow them, how can we disregard their clear example?

- The faith reached us because others cared enough to share it with us – if we are thankful for what we have received, we should pass it on.
- Many churches think of mission as caring for people in ways the outside world will approve of (non-Christians are generally keen on Christian philanthropy and rather less keen on Christians speaking of Jesus), so we have to emphasize the importance of sharing faith. It is often in danger of being crowded out by other concerns.
- Growing numbers are usually, though not always, a sign of health – we should rejoice when churches grow, and certainly not carp.
- Growing numbers involved in church means greater potential for other kingdom work, such as care for the sick, the poor and the marginalized in this country and abroad.

Yes, concern for numbers is not the be-all and end-all. It needs to be balanced with the wider work of the kingdom.

The question for you, as you read this book, is whether in your individual discipleship, and in the local church of which you are a part, you are focused on the internal workings of the church and its philanthropic witness as the main priority, and do you need to give the numerical growth of the church a higher priority?[9]

Brown and Bruce have a point (we will look at the flaws in their analysis later). They highlight the stark reality that inherited forms of Church and the parish system have declined markedly in recent decades and do not touch large swathes of people. In seeking a biblical analogy for the time in which we live, George Lings suggests the analogy of exile, moving from a culture in which

---

9 Jackson, *Hope for the Church*, pp. 17–26.

being Christian was either a given or tolerated, to a culture that is mainly indifferent or hostile. Such an analogy may be unnecessary for Christians who have never known Christian faith as being widely accepted or tolerated. But the analogy of exile resonates in the Christian experience of many.

Part of a right response to exile is repentance and the facing of judgement.[10] The creation in Genesis 1 and 2 is followed in Genesis 3 by the fall of humanity, and that fall is a retreat from the possibility of directly experiencing divine love into stale expressions of self-love, idolatry. Recognizing the reality of human fallenness means we can be clear-eyed about the problems the Church in the West faces. Repentance starts with the Church, made up as it is of fallible men and women. Thus church decline is often explained as a consequence of how individual Christians and Christian communities are – the Church declines because of its many failings. It is so out of touch with culture, so uncaring towards the poor, so lacking in faith and so on.

There is truth in this but also a strong tendency towards masochism in such analysis of the Western Church. Part of the cause of the current woes of the Church are its failings, but these have not suddenly got worse. If its recent decline is due to its sins, then presumably it was far less sinful when it was a lot bigger 150 years ago under Queen Victoria. The Church was numerically much stronger then, yet in a great many ways it was just as fallible – deeply enmeshed with power elites, often racist and often bound up with the wealthy. In some respects the current Church is markedly less sinful than it was in the nineteenth century. Blaming individual Christians and churches for decline is both a skewing of the truth and also pastorally damaging through its demoralizing effect.

Churches need a less masochistic view of themselves. We might start by noting that when people abandon faith or refuse to consider it, this is by no means always or mainly the fault of the Church or of individual Christians. Faith is rejected for many

---

10 G. Lings, 'A Golden Opportunity: Revisiting the Story So Far', *Encounters on the Edge* 50, 2011.

reasons. In a deeply materialist culture, one key reason is consumerism. Moreover, in an age where business, media, government and academic elites wield great power, part of the reason for hostility to Christian faith is structural – a collective unbelief for which the elites are most responsible.

Thus a recent analysis – made before the recent recession – of the worldview of Generation Y, current 15–25-year-olds, concludes that the dominant influences are consumerism, electronic media and globalization. This generation's main aim is personal happiness, and they view the world as benign and life as 'OK'. (Of course, this worldview is shared by many outside this age group and, to a large degree, Generation Y are mirroring the wider culture.) While the Church has much work to do to connect with Generation Y, it is important to recognize that its worldview is close to hedonism and largely indifferent to the needs of the planet. Generation Y's rejection of or indifference towards faith can be seen as much the result of a sinful worldview as of the deficiencies of the Church. Breast-beating by the Church over its own sins obscures the need of all people to repent.[11]

This is not to let the Church off the task of working hard to connect with people, but it's important to stop punishing it, as if secularization was all its fault. For one thing, it makes it sound as if we have only to find the right technique, or try harder, and all will be well – a new version of justification by works. By speaking thus, we act as if the grace of God had no part in the drawing of people to faith; as if individuals had no role in their own coming to faith – in short, we act as if it was all down to us. This is both arrogant, untrue and a recipe for a nervous breakdown. More deeply, it lets contemporary consumerism off far too lightly. A key reason why people have turned from God to wealth is the age-old problem of idolatry. Meaningful spiritual growth will happen not just by making Church attractive but by helping people repent.

---

11 S. Savage, S. Collins-Mayo, B. Mayo with Graham Cray, *Making Sense of Generation Y: The World View of 15–25-Year-Olds*, London: Church House Publishing, 2006.

There is intriguing data suggesting that the more affluent a society becomes, the more secular it becomes. Thus the marked shift to secularization in much of Western and Northern Europe during the 1960s coincided with unparalleled affluence in the West. Oral interviews bring this out well: Jill Barker, from Preston, went to church until she married, but 'When we got married we never bothered', mainly because her husband worked much of the weekends and 'I think we wanted to buy new things, didn't we, and that were the thing: we wanted carpets and stair carpets and new furniture.' One Lancastrian man put the issue succinctly: 'It's an odd thing about deprivation, but it does actually bring people together, far more than affluence does. Affluence, actually, I always feel, divides.'[12] Writing a few months after the 2011 riots across Britain lends this quotation added poignancy. Insofar as churches tend to decline in affluent countries (and there is strong evidence for this in Western and northern Europe), then they should beware simply of blaming themselves for this shift, not least because it allows the idolatrous worship of wealth to go unchallenged.

Judgement, like repentance, starts with the Church before it goes anywhere else. It is a doctrine noticeable for its absence in much of contemporary Christian discourse. The love of God remains rightly central to Christian discourse, but a true depiction of God's love is only possible when paired with a depiction of his justice. Part of any renewal of the Church will come with a fresh recognition that to reconnect with the love of God we must face God's judgement – and the way, in Christ, he bears that judgement himself. A fresh depth of confession is a foundation for the refreshing of the Church. This will be clear-eyed, recognizing where Christians individually and collectively have gone astray, but also facing where the wider culture has become idolatrous.

---

12 H. McLeod, *The Religious Crisis of the 1960s*, Oxford: Oxford University Press, 2007, pp. 111, 171.

## Challenges to the secularization thesis

Moreover, while Christians need to face the full force of secularization, they should not be overwhelmed by it. Taken neat, the secularization thesis creates a kind of eschatology of despair, where all Christians hope for is to hang on in quiet desperation. But the secularization thesis is not all that can be said about the contemporary Church. The most fundamental problem with the thesis is that insofar as it works, it only works in a small number of countries.

Christians from outside Western Europe have had widespread experience of growth, not decline, in recent decades. The last century has seen dramatic shifts – most notably in China, where a Church heavily dependent on missionaries then faced severe persecution under Mao and yet has grown remarkably. Hugh McLeod, a leading historian of Christianity, comments that Christianity in China is 'the biggest question mark' for the future of the Christian faith. China, which may come to dominate the twenty-first century economically, has at the same time become a key centre of Christian faith.[13]

The notion that Western societies in particular are predisposed to be secular is undermined by the experience of the USA: the most modern state remains remarkably religious. Tony Carnes' and Anna Karpathakis' remarkable *New York Glory* charts the extraordinary fertility of churches in that most modern of cities. What is significant for this discussion is that American Christianity gives the lie to the notion that Christianity in the West is bound to decline. Problems with the secularization thesis can also be found closer to home. While much European Christianity has declined in recent decades, non-Christian faiths have mushroomed across Europe. Moreover, while the secularization thesis has some purchase on Western and Northern Europe, it is decidedly less convincing in parts of Southern and Eastern Europe, where churches have either remained strong or even grown.

This has led to alternative theories. Most influential is Rational Choice Theory, which argues that monopolistic established

---

13 McLeod, *World Christianities*, p. 646.

churches tend to grow flabby and decline, while churches facing a pluralist culture are forced to adapt and thereby are more likely to thrive. While this theory has problems, it does help explain why the established churches in Scandinavia and Germany are in drastic decline whereas many churches in the USA are not.[14]

In short, the secularization thesis has some value for some churches in some parts of Western Europe. In most of the globe and in a substantial slice of Europe, it is seriously misleading. Christians have on occasion internalized such sociological doom-mongering when they can afford to be more positive. The tides of belief and unbelief ebb and flow. So with an eye to the global experience of Christian faith, can we see church growth in Britain today?

## Church growth in Britain today

The above debates are valuable but we need to clarify what has been happening in Britain in recent decades. There is a good argument for saying that Christians are more ignorant of their recent past than of their ancient history. There is startling research on recent Christian history that needs to be better known – it has severely dented the claims of the secularization thesis even with regard to Britain by showing that widespread, sustained church growth is taking place.[15] Brown and Bruce may be correct to say that some churches are in deep decline but they ignore the fact that many are growing.

Church growth in Britain has six key facets: growth among ethnic minorities; growth among new churches; growth in cathedrals; growth in London; growth among Baptist churches; and growth through fresh expressions and pioneer ministries.

---

14 R. Finke and R. Stark, *The Church of America 1776–1990: Winners and Losers in Our Religious Economy*, New Brunswick: Rutgers University Press, 2005. For an assessment of this theory see: G. Davie, *A Sociology of Religion*, London: Sage, 2007, pp. 67–88.

15 Goodhew, *Church Growth in Britain*.

## Church growth among ethnic minorities

The diversification of the British population in recent decades is well understood. What is less recognized is that the growth of multi-ethnic Britain has led to a substantial growth in British churches. Around one million people from ethnic minorities are Christians in contemporary Britain. Of these around 500,000 worship in black-led churches. Such growth can be spectacular – as in the case of the Nigerian Pentecostal Redeemed Christian Church of God, which has opened around 400 congregations in the UK since the mid-1980s. Such growth spans an extraordinary variety of nationalities. While black churches are perhaps the most visible sign of such growth, the huge influx of workers from Poland during the last decade has a religious as well as an ethnic dimension. The archetypal Polish plumber brings not just his skills with him but also his faith. This has led to the phenomenon known as 'reverse mission', where some mainline churches are being reinvigorated by migrants into the UK. Thus the Catholic parish of Canning Town in East London has seen a rapid rise in attendance, hosting around 1,200 worshippers weekly, drawn from over 40 nationalities. Such vitality has found expression in new extra-liturgical devotions to the Virgin Mary and new political initiatives, as well as in many other ways. The most visible example of reverse mission is John Sentamu, the Ugandan-born Anglican Archbishop of York. That the second most senior leader of the Church of England should have been born and raised in the heart of Africa is testimony to how previous patterns of mission have gone into reverse in recent decades. Attempts by the far right to demonize ethnic minorities are abhorrent for many reasons – but when such groups as the BNP claim that ethnic minorities undermine the Christian faith, they are not only highly dubious but also highly incorrect. It may well be that Christians from ethnic minorities will be the salvation of the British churches.[16]

---

16 R. Burgess, 'Nigerian Churches in the UK: The Redeemed Christian Church of God', in Goodhew, *Church Growth in Britain*; R. Warner, *Secularization and its Discontents*, London: Continuum, 2010.

## Freedom Centre International, Peckham

Freedom Centre International is a large new Pentecostal church in Peckham. Its founders came from Ghana, and such roots are crucial to its continuing identity. What is striking about FCI is not only its dynamic and large-scale ministry in a multi-ethnic inner city area of London, but the way it has recently started a new congregation in the somewhat leafier suburb of Welling. Welling is all the more interesting a site for a new church given that it was close to the place where the notorious murder of the black teenager, Stephen Lawrence, took place in 1993. FCI has taken over the local cinema in Welling – a striking illustration of the way black-led churches – and ethnic minority Christianity in general – are changing the religious ecology of Britain.[17]

## Church growth among new churches

When commentators refer to 'the Church' they usually mean the mainline churches – Anglican, Methodist, Roman Catholic and so on. There have always been other churches but these are usually treated as too small to merit comment. During the twentieth century there was a proliferation of such churches – often, but not always, as a result of the rise of Pentecostalism and the charismatic movement. What is little recognized is that this proliferation has continued and, if anything, increased in pace during recent decades. The number of Elim Pentecostal churches grew from 437 to 592 during the 1990s alone. New Frontiers – originally part of the 1970s 'house church' movement – now has hundreds of congregations across the UK. Orthodox congregations too have mushroomed since the 1960s. A study of a single city, York, shows that around one congregation a year has been started in that city during the last 30 years – most coming from outside

17 A. Duffour, 'Moving Up and Moving Out: Peckham', in Goodhew (ed.), *Church Growth in Britain.*

the mainline churches. Mainline church members need to have the humility to ask why such churches have been able to grow amid the chill winds of secularization when so many mainline churches have shrunk.

## Growing churches in the UK[18]

|  | 2000 | 2005 | 2010 |
|---|---|---|---|
| Orthodox (membership) | 278,154 | 314,667 | 333,630 |
| 'Mainline' Pentecostal (membership) | 223,464 | 286,929 | 354,934 |
| 'New' churches (Sunday attendance) | 170,259 | 189,873 | 223,290 |

### York Community Church

York Community Church (YCC) started in 1993. Since then it has rooted itself in the rundown suburb of York called Tang Hall. Close to both of York's universities, it has many student members and has grown to a total of 200 adults and 55 children. The church combines a stress on evangelism and wider forms of mission together with a broadly evangelical–charismatic spirituality.[19]

## Church growth in cathedrals

There is a counterpoint to new church growth. Growth is happening at the opposite end of the ecclesiological spectrum, in Anglican cathedrals. Lynda Barley has studied this trend, which

---

18 Brierley (ed.), *Religious Trends 7, 2007–8*, tables 2.22.4, 9.10.1, 9.14.1. These figures should not be read as a precise measure, though they indicate a clear trend.

19 D. Goodhew, 'From the Margins to the Mainstream: New Churches in York', Goodhew (ed.), *Church Growth in Britain*.

has been noticeable across the last two decades. There has been a gentle rise in attendance at Sunday services, combined with a marked rise during weekday worship over the past decade. At the regular services held in cathedrals (excluding Sundays), the average weekly attendance has risen from 4,900 in 2000 to 11,600 in 2010. Much – possibly most – of this increase is the result of one-off acts of worship, the regular congregations showing much more modest growth. More research is needed into what precisely is happening. However, the experience of cathedrals is a striking reminder that supposedly old-fashioned formal worship and traditional language has a significant purchase on the contemporary world. *For the Parish* is right to stress the vitality of traditional worship, but it should be noted that the growth of cathedrals has happened amid widespread decline of traditional worship elsewhere. Some of the growth of cathedral congregations could be happening at the expense of local parishes.

---

### Bradford Cathedral

Bradford Cathedral had some difficult years at the beginning of the millennium. The attendance figures – including attendance at all services, Sunday and weekday, and one-off services – reflect this, but also substantial growth in recent years. The figures are 2000: 314; 2005: 214; 2010: 610.

Sustained work in the city and diocese began to bring organizations into the cathedral for special services, such as 600 Scouts starting to come on St George's Day, the creation of new carol services and so on. There was a further jump in 2010 in the number of such one-off events, up to 51 services from 28 in 2009.

The number of individual worshippers has not risen so strongly: a steady stream of newcomers has been balanced by older members who have died, moved away or become too frail to attend. Nonetheless the electoral roll has increased in the last five years from about 150 to 200. David Ison, the Dean, explains it this way:

> I think that this represents two things: one is the greater openness of organizations to having a spiritual dimension to, and affirmation of, their life together. The other is that more individuals are willing to come with a familiar group and to come to a cathedral where they have some relationship [with what happens there, either through personal contact with a member of the cathedral's community, or through being involved in the life of the city.] It's a bit of a good news story: people who come and enjoy it tell their friends.[20]

Holy Trinity Brompton (often known as HTB) is a large parish church in central London heavily influenced by the charismatic movement. It has planted several dozen new congregations over the past decade. Prior to the Norman Conquest, minster churches were strong centres of Christian faith that promoted new churches in the surrounding area. HTB is acting as a 'minster' for London and beyond. St Paul's Cathedral and Westminster Abbey have seen large congregations attracted to their traditional brand of Anglicanism but do not actively plant new congregations in the choral tradition or actively revitalize dwindling congregations from that tradition. The growth of cathedral congregations validates Davison's and Milbank's view that the traditional parish has a lot of life in it. But the restriction of that growth to cathedrals is a challenge to cathedrals to plant new congregations and revitalize dwindling congregations – thereby fulfilling their vocation as modern minsters.

---

20 Information kindly supplied by Lynda Barley and David Ison.

## Church growth in London

Research concerning Anglican churches shows significant variations in rates of growth and decline. The geographical area seeing the most dramatic growth in recent years is the diocese of London. Bob Jackson's pioneering work showed that adult Sunday attendance in the diocese of London's Anglican churches grew by 12 per cent during the 1990s and that the adult membership (as measured by electoral roll figures) grew by over 70 per cent between 1990 and 2010. In some areas – notably central London – the rise was even more marked. What is happening among Anglicans is being observed in other denominations in London. Likewise new church growth and ethnic minority church growth appears to be strongest in the capital.

Much more research is needed but there does seem to be a correlation between areas of population growth and economic growth and areas of church growth. In the UK, churches are growing most strongly in London and the surrounding areas and declining most rapidly in areas where population is stagnant or falling and where the economy is struggling – such as parts of West Scotland, parts of North England and the valleys of South Wales. It would be wrong to create a crude determinism out of this geographical pattern – there are plenty of shrinking churches in London and growing churches in Scotland, Wales and the North. That growing churches are concentrated in areas of economic dynamism does not mean that the churches themselves are filled with the wealthy – there is a significant correlation between poverty and church growth in London. But an awareness of the geography of decline and growth is an important tool of analysis. There is a strong connection between economic dynamism, immigration and church growth.

## St Michael's, Camden Town

In 1996 Fr Nicholas Wheeler arrived at St Michael's Camden Town to find it had been suffering a prolonged near-death experience. The congregation was down to 12, the church building was falling down and permanently locked, and the church hall had been occupied by squatters for the last 12 years. The church, next door to a large supermarket on a main road, was unlocked and made available to visitors each day. Small improvements made it a more attractive worship space; a little garden was created by the side; the church worked with partners to regain and rebuild the hall as a centre for the community; relationships were repaired with the local school and a Sunday School commenced. Friendly invitations and welcomes, helped by the open church being manned through the week, and by the new priest getting known in the parish, meant that new people kept on arriving on Sundays. New ethnic groups began to find a home there, including a number of different groups of asylum seekers who were quickly given reponsibilities in the church. Two non-stipendiary ministers have been ordained and there is a pastoral assistant focusing on community ministry. Under the new priest, Fr Philip North, the current Mission Action Plan is prioritizing a transition from pioneer clerical leadership to corporate leadership. This church also has a large banner on the outside with its strapline: 'Making a family out of strangers'. By now around 30 nationalities are represented in a worshipping community of around 300 people. Yet average Sunday attendance is only around 100, partly because so many of the congregation work on many Sundays. Although the church now has a functioning toilet, it still has no heating – the current phase of rebuilding should greatly enhance the ability of the church to attract and hold a congregation.[21]

21 John Wolffe and Bob Jackson, 'Anglican Resurgence: The Church of England in London', in Goodhew, *Church Growth in Britain*.

## Church growth among Baptist churches

Most mainline denominations have seen significant decline in recent years, except the Baptists. Baptist churches have held steady overall and in many places grown.[22] This is in startling contrast with other churches – especially similar non-conformist churches such as the URC and the Methodist Church, which are in steep decline. Why is this?

Among a variety of reasons, Baptist churches have seen church planting and other new forms of church as central to their mission since the 1980s. It should also be noted that Baptist churches have always retained an anti-establishment identity. This crystallized around its stress on baptism being the choice of the person being baptized as opposed to infant baptism – a conscious choice by the individual. However, it is reinforced by a wariness of connection with the state. Other denominations more strongly countercultural in the past have become more mainstream and stressed participation in national life. By contrast, Baptist churches have not. It may be that as elite culture pushes Christianity towards the margins, those denominations that are strongly countercultural by nature have better-honed survival strategies than those that wish to be part of the mainstream and now find that they are no longer welcome there. As Christianity in Britain increasingly finds itself 'in exile', the Baptists, who have long operated as if they *are* in exile, have a head-start over many other churches. Baptist churches have a strongly democratic structure of governance, where the congregation has to approve and pay for their pastor. Whether the resilience of Baptist Christianity, compared to Methodism or Anglicanism, is partly due to governance is unclear. However, it could be that such a system leaves Baptist churches less vulnerable to shifts in elite culture that affect Anglicanism or bureaucratic stagnation that has been a besetting problem for Methodism.

---

22 I. Randall, 'Bucking Nonconformist Decline: Baptist Churches 1980–2010', in Goodhew, *Church Growth in Britain*.

## Church planting and the Baptist denomination

In 1992 it was calculated that in the period since 1980, Baptists across the various Areas of the Baptist Union had been involved in the planting of 183 new churches. The Southern Area led the field (37 new churches), followed by the North West (22), then the North East and London (19 each), the South East (17) and the Eastern Area (16). The other Areas averaged a dozen newly planted churches each. The fresh expressions movement is really the latest manifestation of a longer-term trend of starting new churches in Britain that can be found across a number of denominations. What is striking about the Baptists is that this emphasis was adopted earlier and more vigorously than by the other mainline denominations.[23]

## *Church growth through fresh expressions and pioneer ministry*

There have been many new initiatives among Christian churches in recent decades. The notion of church planting began to emerge in the 1970s and gathered steam over the next 20 years. By 2000, hundreds of such 'plants' had been formed and some have grown to substantial entities. In the Anglican Church alone it is reckoned that, added together, those who worship at such 'plants' are equivalent to an average-sized diocese. In 2004, the Anglican report *Mission-Shaped Church* (MSC), highlighted 12 different types of fresh expressions of Church. This in turn has fed into the promotion of 'pioneer ministers' as a means of starting and nurturing such forms. The report has been influential. Research shows that around 1,000 fresh expressions have started since 2004.

More generally, there is consistent evidence that churches that start new forms of Church are far more likely to grow than those

---

23 Randall, 'Bucking Nonconformist Decline'.

that do not.[24] But research shows variation between them, and a significant minority – perhaps up to 20 per cent – have subsequently died out. MSC outlined 12 types of fresh expressions. Since its publication it is clear that some types have been more effective than others. Traditional Church plants, 'cell church' and network churches have shown the greatest vitality. Fresh expressions that are a form of alternative worship have proved effective as generators of creativity but limited in effectiveness as mission.[25] Base (or Basic) Ecclesial Communities were cited as an example of a fresh expression in 2004 but remain extremely rare in England. There is a strong correlation between fresh expressions that are well staffed and fresh expressions that flourish.

---

### Warham – a rural fresh expression

Warham in Hampshire featured in the original MSC report as an example of a fresh expression in a deeply rural context. In an area of Hampshire where your neighbour could be miles away, a church has arisen through Alpha courses in the 1980s. The diocese of Winchester authorized a redundant hamlet church as a centre for midweek training and monthly Sunday services. Tim Humphrey was appointed as Warham Missioner in 1997 and established the Warham Community, which resourced dozens of Alpha courses. Community members and converts were organized in dispersed cells across a 20-mile radius, grouped into three regions for periodic celebrations. Various midweek events were held, such as Alpha courses, marriage and parenting courses. Further growth occurred under new Missioners. An increased desire to serve the wider communities led to the decision to move Sunday services to the afternoon, releasing many people to their local churches, while still having the

---

24 Jackson, *Hope for the Church*, pp. 132–45.

25 G. Lings, 'The Enigma of Alternative Worship', *Encounters on the Edge 12*, 2001. See also the websites of alternative worship communities such as Visions in York, Grace in Ealing and Sanctus 1 in Manchester, accessed 21 September 2011.

opportunity to maintain relationships that had become so important. In 2009 Warham Trust became the Warham Community Church. As a new leadership structure was introduced, Elders were recommended and recognized and a system for membership Partnership was approved. In July 2010 it was decided to cease Sunday meetings and concentrate on providing an opportunity to bring friends along to midweek meetings held in various locations throughout Hampshire and West Berkshire.[26]

These six signs of growth in British churches profoundly subvert the secularization thesis. It is not enough to note decline in general. We must ask which churches are shrinking, in which areas is decline happening and over what timescale. Thus while some mainline churches are in steep decline, Baptist churches are holding steady or growing. While the Anglican Church is declining overall, in the diocese of London it has been growing for the last 20 years. Traditional choral worship is thriving within a cathedral setting, even though it is struggling in many places outside cathedrals. While the majority of mainline churches have declined, new churches and churches of different ethnicities have mushroomed in recent decades. Christianity is healthiest in areas where there is demographic and economic dynamism, such as London; it is exhibiting a startling variety of fresh expressions. A comparison of the number of churches closing and the number opening over the last three decades shows that the number of churches in Britain is roughly the same.

Christianity in Britain is very far from doomed – but it is changing. It is facing significant decline – and growth. All this is in tune with the global Church which, while it is struggling in much of Western Europe, is seeing marked growth in many other contexts.

---

26 *Mission-Shaped Church*, pp. 118–19; www.warhamchurch.org.uk.

## Reprogramming for contemporary Christians

Many British Christians are unaware of these signs of life. A Brazilian friend who moved to this country commented on the resignation he experienced among British Christians. It is likely that the dominant secular culture has entered the collective and individual psyche of British Christians. We need 'reprogramming' so that we cease to be weighed down by the false pessimism of the secularization thesis. We also need to recognize the ways in which churches are growing – and have the humility to learn from them.

---

### Seven-point reprogramming for contemporary Christians

1 *A recognition that church growth is possible and that decline is not inevitable*. The secularization thesis is at best only partly true. The eschatology of decline and its consequent fatalism can therefore be jettisoned and replaced with an eschatology of hope.

2 *A rejection of relativism*, including behavioural relativism, which insidiously affects the Church, encouraging it to treat faith as a lifestyle option not a relationship with the living God. Relativism needs challenging both because it is incompatible with the Christian faith and for the inaction and fatalism towards the status quo that it breeds.

3 *A recognition that church growth is happening overwhelmingly among churches that are unembarrassed by the core doctrines of Christianity*. This is not to say that all such growth is good, nor that orthodox Christianity is free of problems. But such growth shows that there is no warrant for the view that the core doctrines of Christianity have nothing to say to contemporary Britain.

4 *The need for cultural relevance*: churches grow when they listen hard to the surrounding culture in order to relate seriously to it. Such translation does not mean abandonment of tradition, but it does require intelligent adaptation. Those who

stress the value of the traditional parish need to face the evidence that large numbers of traditional parishes are in serious decline – and that significant growth is happening outside traditional structures. Even the culturally conservative Orthodox churches use websites.

5 *The need to be sociologically savvy*: major sociological and economic drivers facilitate or inhibit church growth. This should not mean an abandonment of those areas where growth is most difficult, but it should lead to realism as to the cost of engaging in the most challenging contexts. More broadly, the churches where socio-economic conditions are much more favourable to church growth need to ask how they can support those where growth is proving much harder.

6 *The need to embrace fully ethnic diversity and the new churches*. One of the most startling findings of recent research is the way ethnicity has fed into church growth, but often outside the established denominations. Reprogramming requires, first, a profound recognition by the mainline churches that Christianity rooted in a range of ethnicities has to be embraced in its own terms; second, a new ecumenism that recognizes that the Church is far bigger than the old mainline denominations and that in many places what was 'mainline' is now 'sideline' – and vice versa.

7 *The need to be in it for the long haul*. This volume shows that churches can and often do grow in contemporary Britain, but they only grow in a lasting way if the work of growing the Church is conducted for the long haul. Davison and Milbank are right to be concerned at ephemeral forms of Church. Endurance is essential to its future.

## Conclusion: hope for the Church in exile

> Thus says the Lord GOD: 'I am going to open your graves, and bring you up from your graves, O my people.' (Ezek. 37.12)

So where are we? George Lings suggests that churches in Britain see themselves 'in exile' in a way analogous to the Israelites in Babylon. Our exile consists not of being conquered and deported but of being rejected or ignored. British churches have experienced very significant decline, coupled with a wider secularization of society. As a consequence, large sections of the population have little or no connection with the Christian faith. Part of being in exile is about facing judgement and responding in repentance. The Church needs to repent and it needs to call others to repent. But it doesn't stop there. As the prophet Ezekiel declared, repentance leads into renewal and restoration. Such renewal involves re-imagination. The Israelites had to work out how to worship in a strange land and seek the good of the city in which they found themselves.[27]

MSC is right to point to the huge need for mission in a society that has rapidly secularized – and *For the Parish* is right to point to the significant potential of traditional forms of Church. There is much common ground between these documents. Good parish ministry always recognized that we must 'go to them' not wait for them to 'come to us'. In other words, we must be 'sent', be apostolic. That means there is a huge need for church planting and fresh expressions – fresh expression of traditional and less traditional forms of Church. In some measure all church leaders need to be pioneers, not just a dedicated few. Theological training requires both a deep engagement with the Christian tradition *and* training in how to nurture new churches rather than just maintain existing ones.

Being apostolic in the present day means connecting with 'the parish' or the 'circuit' as it is and will be, rather than as it was. The good news is that there are many examples where the Holy

---

27 Lings, 'Golden Opportunity'.

Spirit is moving ahead of us. As soon as we look beyond Western Europe there is much encouragement, and even within the UK there is evidence of significant and long-term church growth.

*If God can use others, what might he do with you?*

## Further reading

Archbishops' Council, *Mission-Shaped Church*, London: Church House Publishing, 2004.

Brierley, P. (ed.), *Religious Trends 7, 2007–8: British Religion in the Twenty-First Century*, Swindon: Christian Research, 2008.

Brown, C., *The Death of Christian Britain*, London: Routledge, 2001.

Bruce, S., *God is Dead: Secularization in the West*, Oxford: Blackwell, 2002.

Davie, G., *A Sociology of Religion*, Sage, 2007.

Davison, A. and Milbank, A., *For the Parish: A Critique of Fresh Expressions*, London: SCM Press, 2010.

Finke, R. and Stark, R., *The Churching of America, 1776–1990: Winners and Losers in our Religious Economy*, New Brunswick: Rutgers University Press, 2005.

Goodhew, D. (ed.), *Church Growth in Britain from 1980 to the Present Day*, Aldershot: Ashgate, 2012.

Jackson, B., *Hope for the Church*, London: Church House Publishing, 2002.

Jackson, B., 'Hope for the North?', paper given at 'Church:North' conference, 25 February 2011, Cranmer Hall, Durham.

Karnes, T. and Karpathakis, A., *New York Glory*, New York: New York University Press, 2001.

Lings, G., 'A Golden Opportunity: Revisiting the Story So Far', *Encounters on the Edge* 50, 2011.

McLeod, H., 'Being a Christian at the End of the Twentieth Century', in H. McLeod (ed.), *World Christianities c.1914–c.2000, Cambridge History of Christianity*, vol. IX; Cambridge: Cambridge University Press, 2006.

McLeod, H., *The Religious Crisis of the 1960s*, Oxford: Oxford University Press, 2007.

Warner, R., *Secularization and its Discontents*, London: Continuum, 2010.

# 3

# Fresh Expressions:
# What They Are and What
# They Are Not

## Introducing fresh expressions

The term 'fresh expression' has become very widely used across
the Church in the UK in a remarkably short space of time. In 2004,
*Mission-Shaped Church* (MSC) used it to describe new forms of
Church in mission.[1] The report caught the imagination of a wide
cross section of the Church of England and has gone on to sell
over 30,000 copies. The influence of MSC spread quickly to other
denominations[2] and other countries. The Chair of the working
party that produced MSC and now Archbishops' Missioner and
Team Leader of Fresh Expressions, Bishop Graham Cray, would
suggest that this widespread embracing of the report's conclusions was indicative of the Church catching hold of a wave of the
Holy Spirit – a view shared by Tom Stuckey who, in his year as
President of the British Methodist Conference in 2005/6, argued
that 'The Holy Spirit is rattling our bones!'[3]

---

1 Church of England Mission and Public Affairs Council, *Mission-Shaped
Church*, 2nd edn, London: Church House Publishing, 2009, p. 43.

2 While MSC was officially a report the Church of England Mission and Public
Affairs Council, the Methodist Church was represented within the working group by
Revd Graham Horsley, then Secretary for Evangelism and Church Planting within
the British Methodist Church. The 2008 British Methodist Conference commended
the report to the Methodist people for study and discussion alongside the Methodist
statement *Called to Love and Praise* and the documents: 'Our Calling' and 'Priorities
for the Methodist Church'.

3 T. Stuckey, 'The God who inspires', inaugural speech as President of the

Fresh expressions are emerging in all manner of contexts. Many reflect Luke's cameo portrait of the life of the early Church in Acts 2.42–47.[4] Hallmarks typically include a deep sense of commitment and community. Prayer and a desire to discern God's will are central. Open heartedness and a readiness to serve are often apparent. Creativity and imagination are characteristic, especially in corporate worship. Hospitality is a key value and many fresh expressions gather around food.

James Dunn, commentating on the passage, suggests that we should not be surprised.

> The portrayal may be somewhat idealized . . . But anyone who is familiar with movements of enthusiastic spiritual renewal will recognize authentic notes: the enthusiasm of the members of the renewal group, with a sense of overflowing joy (2.46), desire to come together frequently (2.44, 46), eating together and worshipping (2.46–47) and including the readiness for unreserved commitment to one another in a shared common life.[5]

When the Spirit of God stirs the Church we see renewed life and mission; transformation within and without.

Two other key characteristics of fresh expressions are worth noting at this stage. The first is that they take theology seriously. While some are blessed with the tools of academic theology, many are not; but that does not mean that they do not think deeply about God, mission and Church. Commenting on their experience of Fridays in Faith in Annan, John Drane and Olive Fleming-Drane wrote:

> Key Christian themes – often following the seasons and Christian festivals – are explored through many different media that are carefully chosen so as to be inclusive of all the age groups represented. The way that Christian truth is integrated through

Methodist Conference, 2005, www.methodist.org.uk/index.cfm?fuseaction=opento god.content&cmid=1100.

4 See A. Roberts, 'The Acts of the Apostles: Resourcing and Developing Fresh Expressions of Church', *Epworth Review* 36.3, 2009.

5 J. Dunn, *The Acts of the Apostles*, Peterborough: Epworth Press, 1996, p. 34.

such diverse activities is commendable not only for its creativity and imagination, but also for its theological sophistication, which is of a very high order indeed.[6]

New theological insights are emerging in fresh expressions, and as questions are rightly asked of them, so similar questions are being asked of all forms of Church.

The second interesting characteristic is that many fresh expressions are deeply sacramental both in a specific sense – having a high regard for the sacraments of baptism and holy communion – and in a general sense as they seek to be grace-filled communities that are living outward signs of God's goodness and love. When Barbara Glasson was leading the bread-making church Somewhere Else, I asked her about the place of Holy Communion in that community. She explained that 'Holy Communion is not something we do, it is who we are'. They did celebrate the specific sacrament but they saw their whole life together as being thankful, broken, blessed and shared. We explore the sacramental nature of fresh expressions more in the next chapter.

## A new move of mission

*Mission-Shaped Church* released a new movement of imaginative missionary thinking and activity across a wide spectrum of churches and denominations. One of the most striking features of the fresh expressions movement is how it has transcended spectrums of demography, geography, theology, church tradition and denomination. While MSC has been critiqued for being too urban (Smith, 2008), too evangelical (Hull, 2007), too American (theologically – Davison and Milbank, 2010), the fresh expressions movement it gave birth to is marked by diversity. There are fresh expressions working with all ages from toddlers to octogen-

6 'Reformed, Reforming, Emerging and Experimenting: A Study in Contextual Theology Reflecting the Experiences of Initiatives in Emerging Ministry being Funded by the Church of Scotland', p. 48. The report was commissioned by the Church of Scotland Ministries Council and the Mission and Discipleship Council in 2010 to form the basis of a report to the General Assembly in 2011.

arians and many with a full mix of ages. Fresh expressions can be found in small rural communities, inner city centres, seaside towns and leafy suburbs. From his extensive research into church planting and fresh expressions George Lings argues strongly that fresh expressions are to be found in a great range of contexts and that 'It is simply not true that fresh expressions are a middle-class, middle-England phenomenon.'[7]

Those leading fresh expressions range theologically from the conservative to the radical. There are catholic, charismatic, monastic and evangelical fresh expressions and those that would not wear any of these labels. This is a diverse movement. And it is this diversity in particular that suggests we may be truly seeing something of the *missio Dei* unfold. If fresh expressions were only forming in one way or as an adjunct of one tradition, the cynics might be entitled to say, 'Well they would do it that way, wouldn't they.'

The mission-shaped/fresh expressions movement is being embraced by and impacting on people across spectrums that so often divide both Christians and cultures. The Spirit of God cannot be boxed in and domesticated. The wind blows wherever it will (John 3.8), and the wind of the Spirit is blowing through and beyond the Church to make the love of God known to all sorts of people in all sorts of places. Fresh expressions are just one way in which Christians are seeking to join in with what God is doing in these days.

There are some notable exceptions to the rule of diversity. To date there has been no significant Roman Catholic or Orthodox Church involvement. Some but by no means all new church streams have engaged with the vision at national and local level. Most notably the involvement of Christians and churches of non-white British ethnicities is markedly limited so far. There are some very good examples of fresh expressions among these ethnicities, including Sanctuary[8] in Birmingham and Adrenalin in Leicester,[9]

---

7 G. Lings, 'A Golden Opportunity: Revisiting the Story So Far', *Encounters on the Edge* 50, 2011, p. 12.

8 www.eastandwest.co.uk/sanctuary.

9 www.freshexpressions.org.uk/stories/adrenalin.

but they are comparatively few in number. There is at least one positive reason for this: many predominantly non-white British churches are growing strongly in the UK anyway, so the need for fresh expressions may be less apparent but, if the fresh expressions movement is to be truly and fully cross-cultural, relationships with non-white majority British churches will need to be more fully developed.

## The Fresh Expressions team

In 2004 the British Methodist Conference identified the 'encouraging of fresh ways of being church'[10] as one of its five key strategic priorities, citing MSC as a 'valuable resource which will help us grasp the scope of what might be entailed in "new ways of being church"'[11]. The Conference report also went on to replace the phrase 'fresh ways of being Church' with 'fresh expressions of Church'.[12] Given this synergy of vision, it was natural and fitting that the fresh expressions movement began ecumenically.

To support this new move of mission the Fresh Expressions team was founded in 2004 by the Archbishops of Canterbury and York and the Methodist Council. The team is itself supported by a partnership of denominations, streams and mission organizations. Denominational and stream partners include the Church of England, the British Methodist Church, Ground Level Network, the United Reformed Church and the Congregational Federation. Partner mission agencies include Anglican Church Planting Initiatives, Church Army, the Church Missionary Society, the 24/7 prayer movement and YWAM. At the time of writing, conversations are being held with other potential denominational partners. Good relationships with the Church of Scotland and the Baptist Union are already in place, both denominations being involved with the Fresh Expressions team at a local level.

As the movement spreads, equivalent organizations are being

---

10 *Over to You 2004: Reports from the Methodist Conference*, Peterborough: Methodist Publishing House, 2004, p. 2.

11 *Over to You*, p. 9.

12 *Over to You*, pp. 9, 10.

formed in other countries. The first to be formed was Fresh Expressions Canada.[13] The United States, Australia, New Zealand and Barbados have formed fresh expressions bodies to encourage and support the development of new missional churches. There are also developments in Continental Europe, where major Conferences have been held in Germany and Scandinavia. As in the UK, there is a particular challenge to engage with non-white and non-Western cultures. The developing relationship between Fresh Expressions UK and churches in the Caribbean is a hopeful sign that this move of mission can indeed be for all ethnicities. As the international partnerships grow, so learning is flowing back to the UK. This brings a sense of the movement going full circle, given that one of the seminal texts that has inspired it is Vincent Donovan's *Christianity Rediscovered*, in which the Catholic missionary shares the insights he learnt about cross-cultural mission and culturally authentic Church.

## How does Fresh Expressions the team define fresh expressions the new church communities?

The Fresh Expressions team offers the following definition of a fresh expression of Church, recognizing that it is provisional:

> A fresh expression is a form of Church for our changing culture established primarily for the benefit of people who are not yet members of any church.

- It will come into being through principles of listening, service, incarnational mission and making disciples.
- It will have the potential to become a mature expression of Church shaped by the gospel and the enduring marks of the Church and for its cultural context.[14]

The Share the Guide website helpfully provides a focused version of this complex definition, stating that fresh expressions are:

---

13 www.freshexpressions.ca.
14 Fresh Expressions, Prospectus, vol. 2.

- missional
- contextual
- formational
- ecclesial.[15]

There is a lively and ongoing debate as to how many new initiatives fulfil all of the definitional criteria. Here we unpack the definition and offer some examples of ways in which fresh expressions are living out the four key words.

## Missional

Fresh expressions are intentionally missional, outward-looking Christian communities called into being to make the love of God known in an increasingly secular society among the majority of the population who have no significant relationship with the Church and little or no knowledge of Jesus Christ and the Christian faith. They have a deep sense of being sent, of apostolicity.

In 2010, The Welcome at Knutsford in Cheshire was officially recognized as a Methodist church, complete with its own Church Council, 15 years after Deacon Sue Jackson had first walked around a needy estate, talking to people, getting to know them and finding out what they needed. The call was for second-hand clothing, so Sue started to provide facilities – usually the boot of her car – for people to bring and buy clothes.

As demand grew, a lease was taken on what was originally a doctor's surgery, and that became a Christian place to sell clothing and serve coffee. Sue moved on to be replaced by a second deacon, Margaret Fleming. A fresh expression began to develop. There had always been a Christian ethos of meeting people where they were, but increasingly the people themselves began to ask why the church was doing this. As the church

---

15 www.sharetheguide.org/section1/1.

grew and developed a contextualized worship life alongside the service it offered, the community named the place. They were very clear that they wanted it to be called The Welcome.

After ten years questions were starting to be asked by the community as to why The Welcome was not being officially recognized as a church. Commenting on the official recognition of The Welcome as a church, the Revd Ben Clowes said, 'The important thing is that this has come up from the community; this is the way they want to do church but they also want to be recognized.'[16]

The Welcome continues to grow in both new ways and in maturity as Church, just one of many fresh expressions that is making the love of God known in word and deed and enjoying the goodwill of the people as a result (Acts 2.47).

MSC, in developing its vision for a mixed economy of inherited and fresh expressions of Church, all shaped for mission, drew on research by Philip Richter and Leslie Francis for the *Gone but not Forgotten* report of 1988. The report found that in England:

- 10 per cent of people were regular attenders of a church (at least monthly).
- 10 per cent were occasional attenders.
- 20 per cent were open de-churched.
- 20 per cent were closed de-churched.
- 40 per cent were non- or never-churched (other than attending a funeral, wedding etc).
- Those of other faiths were not included in these figures.

Broadly speaking, 40 per cent of the English population (excluding those of other faiths) were within the missional orbit of existing churches. They either saw themselves as being part of a church or were open to returning to active engagement with the Church. Translated into millions, this is an awful lot of people – enough to keep every parish, circuit and local church busy for a

---

16 www.freshexpressions.org.uk/stories/welcome.

long time. The 20 per cent identified as open de-churched are the people for whom the Back to Church Sunday initiative has been so effective. Within a mixed-economy church there is plenty of missional life and opportunity to be found in inherited churches that are committed to mission, as texts such as MSC, *The Future of the Parish System* and *Reshaping the Mission of Methodism* have made abundantly clear (see Further Reading at the end of this chapter).

Good news, but this leaves 60 per cent of people in England seeing churches as strange places, full of strange people, doing strange things or, in the case of the closed de-churched, as painful places. MSC argued that it is for this 60 per cent of people that fresh expressions are needed. Without them a majority of the population were very unlikely to seek or be found by the Church. The need to connect with this proportion of the population remains at the heart of the fresh expressions vision.

The data presented by Richter and Francis was age sensitive. The older people are, the more likely they are to be able to relate to inherited churches, which again opens up plenty of possibilities. But – and it's a particularly challenging but – the younger people are, the less likely they are to relate to inherited churches of *any* style, tradition or denomination.

In a much larger survey published by Tearfund in 2007 that used a different methodology, the figure for the missional orbit of existing churches had decreased to around 32 per cent.[17] The proportions were different in different parts of the UK (England 31 per cent, Northern Ireland 63 per cent, Scotland 33 per cent, Wales 25 per cent).

The longer definition deliberately says fresh expressions are primarily for the benefit of people who are not yet members of any church. The inclusion of the word 'primarily' recognizes that a fresh expression has to begin with a pioneer or, better still, a small community set aside for that purpose by an existing church. It

---

17 Tearfund report *Churchgoing in the UK 2007*. In the Tearfund research the total population from which the percentages are derived does include those of other faiths, which automatically lowers the percentages of those engaging with the Christian Church.

also allows for those who have remained faithful to an inherited church, sometimes clinging on by their fingernails, and who need a fresh expression themselves if they are to grow further in their faith and be part of a community that they can welcome their non-Christian friends to. Without fresh expression these people can all too easily become part of the group of people that has become known as de-churched – a not altogether helpful term.

## What do we mean by mission?

While mission remains at the forefront of the vocabulary of the contemporary British Church, it is not necessarily the case that all Christians mean the same thing when they use it. For some Christians, mission is all about big kingdom values like justice and peace, while for others it's all about evangelism and church growth. Fresh Expressions partner denominations the Church of England and the United Reformed Church recognize the following five marks of mission:

- to proclaim the Good News of the kingdom
- to teach, baptize and nurture new believers
- to respond to human need by loving service
- to seek to transform unjust structures of society
- to strive to safeguard the integrity of creation and sustain and renew the life of the earth.

The British Methodist Church has a longer list stating that mission is:

- telling the good news of Jesus Christ
- calling people to faith in Jesus Christ and Christian discipleship
- caring for individual people and communities
- sharing in the task of education, and social and spiritual development
- struggling for a just world
- being alongside the poor
- becoming friends with people of different cultures and faiths

- caring for the earth
- building partnerships with other churches and groups who share some of our mission aims.

All three denominations acknowledge that when Christians speak of mission, it is God's Mission – the *missio Dei* – that is foundational. In the beginning God. God breathed life into creation and is ever active, reaching out to redeem and renew creation. God breathed life into the Church at Pentecost to share the missionary work of redemption and renewal. The Church is a fruit of mission – God's reaching out in love – and a sign, instrument and foretaste of the kingdom of God. The theological sequence is critical here. Theology precedes and shapes missiology, which precedes and, together with theology, shapes ecclesiology.

In practical terms this means that when a group of Christians starts to think about forming a fresh expression, the vital first question to ask is, 'What is God like?' The answer will be hugely important for shaping the resultant mission and the Church that forms from it. This thinking needs to be more than a cerebral exercise. It needs to be one of both mind and heart, of seeking to feel the divine heartbeat – asking how does God see or feel about this community, these people, these needs?

Susan came into the high street cafe simply to have a cup of coffee. She was not looking for church. She enjoyed the coffee and the warm atmosphere and came again. She kept on coming, and after a while she started being part of the Wednesday evening worship.

Susan's career background was the sex trade. One Wednesday evening some high-ranking church leaders visited the cafe. Part-way through the worship there was an open-mike time for anyone to share anything they wanted to say. While the work of the Spirit was ever more evident in Susan's life, there were particular parts that were still in need of redemption, not least her choice of language. The minister leading the service was quietly hoping that Susan would not take the mike that evening but, of course, she did. She did not disappoint, beginning by saying, 'My partner is a right \*\*\*\* \*\*\*\*.' Silence descended and then she added, 'But I have never experienced before the love I have experienced here.' She went on to describe how the love of Jesus and his people were changing her life.

Having suffered from alcohol abuse for years, Susan's liver gave way and her new life on this earth was short-lived. At her funeral, as the minister was reading the words, 'The tribulations of this world are over and earth is past', he had a vision of Susan 'dancing in glory'.

For many years and across the denominations there has been a deliberate embracing of a spectrum of understanding of what mission is in practice. Mission is both social and evangelistic. It is about individuals, communities and creation. Mission is holistic. This spectrum of missional understanding and practice is evident both within and across fresh expressions. One of the gifts of fresh expressions to the wider Church may be the discovery of fresh ways in which this holistic understanding of mission can be realized in practice.

Street Church in Northampton welcomes up to 90 vulnerable and homeless people at its weekly get-togethers. A lot of homeless people find Sunday the most difficult day of the week because there is nothing open specifically for them, so local Christians got together to arrange a weekly Street Church drop-in service from 1.30 p.m. to about 3 p.m. Christians from the Church of England, Kingdom Life New Frontiers International Church, the Salvation Army and the Roman Catholic Church all help out.

Multi-media material is used to explore issues from a Christian perspective – usually through visual images rather than words. There is very little 'preaching', more the sharing of testimonies and stories with a lot of one-to-one relational conversations. Guests are invited and sing in what local vicar David Bird describes as 'performance worship'. Some of the homeless people have musical gifts that they share in these times.

Every six weeks or so, pampering is offered, when people get their nails and hair cut. Some women working in the sex trade also come in, and those serving do their nails too, just to serve them and show that they care.

And people come to faith.

The full definition offered by the Fresh Expressions team says that a fresh expression of Church will come into being through incarnational mission, a central theological principle so well captured by *The Message* translation of John 1.14: 'The Word became flesh and moved into the neighbourhood.' Whether those planting a fresh expression are moving into the neighbourhood – or network – or are already part of it, they need to meet Christ in others (Matt. 25.31–40) and to make Christ known in themselves by being or becoming fully part of that context. They need to listen as well as to speak, to receive as well as to give, to share the needs of those they seek to serve.

Because the fresh expressions movement is still comparatively young, evaluations need to be made carefully. Gathering data on how many fresh expressions there are and how many people are part of them is a complex and developing yet urgent task. The Church of England, the Methodist Church and Church Army are all attempting to measure fully what is going on. The 2010 Methodist Church statistics revealed 941 fresh expressions that respondents said matched the definition offered by the Fresh Expressions team. Further research is needed into these figures, but the good news is that 24 per cent of all British Methodist churches and 67 per cent of all British Methodist circuits are living out the connexional priority to encourage fresh expressions. George Lings of the Church Army Research Centre ventures that:

We simply do not know the overall total number of fresh expressions of Church started since the report but estimations of over 1,000 do not appear fanciful. There are signs that certain kinds are prolific. Several dioceses have records of up to 100 alleged examples, although I am sure not all of these are fresh expressions in the terms described in *Mission-Shaped Church*.[18]

A particularly popular form of fresh expression is Messy Church. Inspired by Lucy Moore, this has become a movement in its own right. In 2010 there were an estimated 100,000 people involved in Messy Churches across Britain, and the movement has spread to other countries. Meanwhile there are growing numbers of individual fresh expressions that are showing signs of strong mission-driven growth. Tubestation[19] formed among the surfing community in Cornwall in 2007 now has multiple services during the peak surfing season and is currently seeking to develop its mission in other parts of North Cornwall. Within four years of its launch in 2007, The Wesley Playhouse[20] in Howden Clough had seen over 53,000 people come through its doors. It's a long way from the days when the pre-Playhouse Howden Clough Church had just 10 members attending regularly. Now thought is being given to planting a second Playhouse in the North-East of England. G2 was planted by St Michael le Belfrey, York, in a gym near the university in 2004. The fresh expression has now outgrown the gym, with 100 people regularly at Sunday meetings in a community centre and a total fellowship of around 200 gathering in a variety of small groups, cell groups, clusters, student groups and mums and tots.[21]

Many fresh expressions are comparatively small because they are young. Qualitatively their missional impact is often high. Quantatively there is room for growth. They are in good company

---

18 G. Lings, 'A History of Fresh Expressions and Church Planting in the Church of England', in D. Goodhew (ed.), *Church Growth in Britain from 1980 to the Present Day*, Aldershot: Ashgate, 2012, p. 234. The revised and pruned Sheffield Centre database holds 777 specific records for the overall period 1992–2008.

19 www.tubestation.org.

20 www.freshexpressions.org.uk/stories/playhouse.

21 www.freshexpressions.org.uk/stories/g2.

here. As we noted in Chapter 1, most if not all of the churches that Paul wrote to were still small enough to meet in a home when he wrote, albeit often a large home. But there is a risk that as communities form they can quickly become cosy. The new becomes familiar and comfortable and the desire to welcome others who will inevitably change things simply by being there can diminish as the sense of being sent fades. There is a balance to be achieved between depth of community and growth of community. There is also a balance to be achieved between pastoral and missional needs – two needs that can be presented as a false dichotomy. Reflecting on his time leading Sanctus1 in Manchester, Ben Edson said:

> Once a fresh expression is established it is likely that the pioneer will also have pastoral oversight for the community. Good pastoral care is vital as it affirms and values those who are part of the fresh expression; poor pastoral care is failure in the missional task. It is not mission or pastoral care; it is pastoral care and mission – a well-cared-for fresh expression will be an attractive missional community.
>
> The pioneer therefore needs to balance their resources to make sure that the fresh expression is being pastorally cared for, whilst also making sure that they are leading in mission. There will be times when pastoral care is taking a lot of time and this can lead to frustrations. This is when the pioneer needs to be looking at the long-term picture and recognizing that the community are the primary mission unit rather than the individual. To remain in mission mode the pioneer needs to resource the community in mission and the best way that this can be done is by leading in mission.[22]

What form quantitative growth should take is a matter for reflection and debate. Some fresh expressions, as illustrated above, are showing signs of significant numerical growth, making new disciples and consequently able to have a larger missional footprint in terms of the other marks of mission. Others, particularly many

---

22 Ben Edson, quoted in the *Mission-Shaped Ministry* course unit, 'Growing a Fresh Expression to Maturity'.

of the new monastic communities, are intentionally small to support deep relationships. Still others that are attending to very deep pastoral needs, including addictions, need to be small to offer the environment and support this role requires.

Church growth advocate Bob Jackson makes an interesting contribution to the debate about growth:

> We treated our churches as if they were all oak trees – able to grow to any size and live virtually forever. One plant could fill the whole parish garden more or less permanently. But most congregations are primroses – they have a limited, vigorous individual life, and they grow and spread to fill the ground by division into large numbers of individual plants.[23]

As with all analogies, the primrose has its limitations. To some it may suggest something ephemeral and lacking in substance, here one moment and gone the next. I am no gardener, but I believe primroses are perennials and do reproduce and grow as Bob Jackson suggests, so there is value in his picture, particularly if it is taken to represent a mixed-economy or mixed-ecology church in which the old and the new grow together.

Whether they have a limited or longer life, many fresh expressions are either intentionally small or are made up of small cells. Some workplace-based ones, such as work:space in Poole, are formed of a network of small missional communities, and meet in places like the headquarters of Barclays Bank and the training college of the Royal National Lifeboat Institution.[24] Many fresh expressions have intentionally embraced the vision and values of cell church. Mind the Gap in Gateshead[25] is one such. Still others are choosing to take a monastic approach, with a strong emphasis on community, a meal table as the key meeting place – the Safe Space community in Telford has chosen this way of being Church.[26] For many of these monastic communities (and indeed

23 B. Jackson, *Hope for the Church*, London: Church House Publishing, 2002, p. 132.

24 www.freshexpressions.org.uk/stories/workspace.

25 As featured on *Expressions: The DVD*.

26 www.safespace.me.uk.

some other forms of fresh expressions), small is beautiful, facilitating depth of relationships and discipleship. If such fresh expressions are primroses, then missional growth across the marks of mission will be achieved by their proliferation – planting more primroses, connected together and sitting alongside and working with the long-established oak trees.

## Contextual

Sue Wallace loves Jesus and the ancient traditions of the Christian Church. She also loves clubbing. Wanting to bring together her loves, she worked with a small group of friends to develop Visions at York Minster, a fresh expression seeking to make the love of Jesus known to others who love clubbing. Ancient prayers blend with contemporary dance music. Lighting is provided by candles surrounding a state-of-the-art LCD projector and amid it all, Jesus is offered in the Eucharist.[26] The 'Transcendence Mass' has gone on to plant sister congregations in Beverly and Leeds.

Both MSC and the Methodist text, *Changing Church for a Changing World*,[28] reflected upon the enormous changes occurring at an increasingly rapid rate within British culture and society. These changes have led in many contexts to a gap, a chasm even, opening up between the culture of many churches and those of the communities in which they are set.

While writing this chapter I boarded a crowded commuter train in Birmingham. A group of lively young adults in their twenties got on at the same time and started to unwind from their day's work by chatting and sharing stories. I was trying to read an eru-

27 The story of Visions can be seen on the DVD *Sanctus* produced by Fresh Expressions. It is written up in S. Croft and I. Mobsby (eds), *Fresh Expressions in the Sacramental Tradition*, Norwich: Canterbury Press, 2009.

28 P. Pillinger and A. Roberts, *Changing Church for a Changing World*, Peterborough: Methodist Publishing House, 2007.

dite book on ecclesiology but put it down as the conversation was fascinating, startling, challenging and illuminating all at the same time. Several of the young women starting swapping birth stories, the stories growing ever more gruesome and graphic. The topic then moved on to the BBC programme EastEnders – one of the men said his Mum had stopped watching it since it began to feature a gay couple. This led to a conversation about generational attitudes to gay people, the young adults holding very different ones from their parents. A bizarre discussion then ensued among the women: if they were lesbian, which sort of woman would they fancy? One said she would be a lip-gloss lesbian (new to me) and prefer a partner like Cameron Diaz or Nicole Sherzinger (both of whom I do know, albeit not personally, and neither of whom are lesbians). Then the topic changed to the weekend and the plans to go to a giant school disco at Butlins where the headline act would be Jason Donovan. I looked at my book on ecclesiology and thought: these folk are not on a different page, they are on a different planet. Increasingly for many people who are not active members of the Christian community, Church is simply off their radars. It's not that they're against church or the Christian faith, they simply don't connect with any expressions of them. And it's not their fault.

To connect with an increasingly diverse and distant population, fresh expressions are being formed that create contextually accessible Christian communities. In central Cambridge a Eucharist is celebrated that has been formed in a Goth culture. Graham Cray explains the thinking behind the service:

There is no intention to divide people up. The Goth service does not have black-clad security guards to ban non-Goths at the door. The aim is to plant church into the communities to which people actually belong. Then those churches can reach out to people who are different as well.

This is based on two important biblical principles, both found in 1 Corinthians. First, they assume that when the gospel is preached in a new community, God grows a church, not just wins some individual Christians. Paul says that he planted the gospel seed, others watered it, but God gave the growth and what he grew was the church in Corinth (1 Cor. 3.6–9). He also says that when the new believers were baptized, they were all baptized 'into one body' (12.13).

The second principle is that, just as God's Son entered our world to win us, so Christian missionaries need to enter the cultures they are trying to reach (9.19–23), so that new believers only have to face the stumbling block of the cross (1.18–25), and not the stumbling block of church culture as well! They can then become agents for change within their culture rather than be drawn out of it into a church culture, which may be alien to them.[28]

Planting fresh expressions into cultures that, for whatever reason, are absent or under-represented in most existing churches is no easy task. Two equal and opposite dangers are readily apparent. The first is imperialism – the risk that the founders will impose their cultural preferences on a newly forming church rather than allowing contextually fitting forms of service, learning, worship and evangelism to develop. These cultural preferences may be derived from society or from the structures and practices of denominations or church traditions that once were fitting but may not be now. The second danger is syncretism – the risk that the values, forms and behaviours of a particular cultural context, some of which may be at odds with the gospel, are adopted uncritically in the shaping of the fresh expression.

To avoid these twin dangers a process of 'inculturation' is needed – first named at the Second Vatican Council. When the 'Word became flesh', the logos was still the logos. The ageless essence of God was revealed in the human Jesus expressed in a way

---

29 Adapted with permission from www.freshexpressions.org.uk/about/introduction.

that related to a particular place, time and culture. God incarnate shared fully and authentically in the culture of first-century Palestine. The word became flesh and ate according to local customs, shared in the rituals of the local society and was fully present in homes and workplaces. While Christ lived authentically within and served that culture, he also demonstrated to it the transforming and transcending vision and values of the kingdom of God. When these were embraced, change occurred.

This engagement of fresh expressions with culture is therefore a two-way process of incarnation and reconciliation, redemption and salvation. On the one hand, the fresh expression lives authentically within and serves the culture (incarnation); on the other, the new church, as it lives out the gospel and the values of the kingdom, will bring challenge and change to anything in that culture that dehumanizes and hinders God's kingdom (reconciliation, redemption and salvation). Through this engagement all sorts of fresh insights into missiology, ecclesiology, biblical hermeneutics, worship and discipleship emerge. It is an exciting place to be.

One of the major criticisms of fresh expressions is made of those that focus on a particular culture or group of people. Critics argue that such a focus is counter to an understanding that both the gospel and the Church are for all. At worst we have a contradiction of the high priestly prayer of Jesus in John 17, or a form of spiritual apartheid – things actively unhelpful to mission. Particular opprobrium is reserved by some for the Homogenous Unit Principle developed by Donald McGavran, who declared that people 'like to become Christians without crossing racial, linguistic, or class barriers'.[30] Working from this premise, he argued that for the sake of mission it is best to form churches within the different groups that people are already part of.

This a complex conversation with many layers. It is also a point at which the relationship between missiology and ecclesiology is particularly important. The gospel is for all, but how can it be made known to all? It is precisely because many – perhaps most – churches only engage with a subset of their local population that fresh expressions are needed.

---

30 See *Mission-Shaped Church*, 2nd edn, p. 108.

When the Spirit came at Pentecost, the different people groups – *ethne*s, or cultures – gathered in Jerusalem did not start speaking the same language, rather the disciples were empowered to speak in different languages. This was a godly affirmation of cultural diversity. To make the gospel known today, the Church needs to be present within a great variety of cultures and to be able to speak a great variety of languages, cultural as well as national. If the Church is to connect with people where they are, then Church needs to be where they are, and this calls for a variety of forms of contextualized Church. For as George Lings puts it:

> There is a crucial link between habitat and habits. Everything exists in relation to its environment. This gives another reason to persuade all pioneers and evangelists not to import the model of Church they like (still less those which have become popular) but to follow the genuine mission-shaped process of double listening and to grow what genuinely fits the context, because it grows out of it.[31]

As long ago as 1976, Lesslie Newbigin spoke passionately of the fundamental need for Christian unity, particularly at a local level, but recognized that for the sake of Christ's mission it will be necessary for the gospel to be offered through a range of expressions of Church.

> The existence of separate congregations in the same geographical area on the basis of language and culture may have to be accepted as a necessary, but provisional, measure for the sake of the fulfilment of Christ's mission. Necessary because there must be the possibility to bring to full ripeness the special gifts and insights that God has given to peoples of different language and culture and this cannot happen if some have no place except on the margin of a community of another language or culture. Provisional because the Gospel is the good news of God's purpose,

---

31 Lings, 'Golden Opportunity', p. 13.

to bring all these gifts to their perfection in his new creation where – all together – they will shine in their true glory.[32]

Missiologically, diversity is crucial. However, that is only one side of the coin. Writing on the website Share, Mike Moynagh argues that 'fresh expressions are called to exist in the fragments of society so that they can connect those fragments together'.[33] Unity is also crucial. The Gospel of John presents Jesus as praying passionately for the unity of the Church. That unity is crucial for ecclesiological identity so that the Church may reflect and enjoy the unity that is within the Godhead, 'that they may all be one. As you, Father, are in me and I am in you, may they also be in us'. It is also vital for mission, 'so that the world may believe that you have sent me' (John 17.21). There is an inextricably linked trinity of theology, missiology and ecclesiology underpinning the need for unity. And as George Lings helpfully points out, 'creating fresh expressions is equally a missional and an ecclesial task'.[34]

What is needed across the mixed economy of fresh expressions and inherited churches is a humble view of the local church and a high view of catholicity. A humble view that recognizes that no local church, however big or small, not even Holy Trinity Brompton, Hillsong, Methodist Central Hall Westminster, Tubestation, Moot or Somewhere Else is fully representative of the body of Christ. And a high view of catholicity that recognizes that every church, whether the newest fresh expression or the longest established church in town, has something to contribute to the whole body of Christ and is incomplete without all the other parts of the body, no matter how apparently small, new or insignificant. All churches are *an* expression of *the* Church. Completeness is found in Christ, and until Christ comes again, all churches will continue to be on a journey to full communion with Christ and each other. So the skaters do need the Goths; the Messy Church clientele do need those who meet at 8 a.m. for Book of Common Prayer Communion and vice versa; and so on. In local contexts the mixed

---

32 www.wcc-coe.org/wcc/who/crete-03-e.html.
33 www.sharetheguide.org/section1/2/unity.
34 Lings, 'Golden Opportunity', p. 17.

economy needs to be a living visible reality if the Church is to be as effective in mission as possible. Again to quote Newbigin:

> In order that the Church in each place may be truly the sign, foretaste and instrument of God's purpose of unity, and because there is in each place a plurality of 'places'; because there is a plurality of secular situations within which the Church in each town or city must live and minister; it may be necessary as a provisional arrangement to acknowledge distinct congregations formed primarily (but never exclusively) by those of a distinct language or culture so that the 'local church' takes the form of a plurality of congregations. But such arrangements must be understood as provisional, looking always to the unity which is the promise of the Gospel. This means that there must be: (i) Full mutual recognition by which the distinct congregations accept and welcome one another, recognizing that their separate meeting represents no mutual estrangement but only the acknowledgement of creaturely distinctions of language and culture. (ii) Total freedom of movement between those congregations and a full welcome for members of each at the meetings of all. A provisional arrangement accepted by all as a means of giving freedom for the development of an authentic experience of the Gospel in each particular community is one thing; and enforced apartheid, especially one defended on dogmatic grounds, is quite another. The latter is a direct contradiction of the Gospel. (iii) Structures which are explicitly designed to promote the growth in unity of those who are provisionally separated.[35]

Spoken over 35 years ago, this sounds powerfully contemporary and prophetic. It is also deeply challenging, especially the points about full mutual recognition and total freedom of movement. The picture Newbigin paints would be welcomed by many in the emerging denominations who see themselves as post-denominational.

---

35 www.wcc-coe.org/wcc/who/crete-03-e.html.

## Formational

Fresh expressions are formational. They form disciples, they form leaders and they form communities. To share fully in God's mission they also need to be transformational of the contexts in which they are set and the wider society and wider world of which they are part.

---

Zac's Place began in the late 1990s when Sean Stillman moved to South Wales and conducted a couple of funerals for members of motorcycle clubs, who in turn began to ask very deep questions and wanted to know more about God, but couldn't see how mainstream church was relevant to them.

So Sean booked a function room in a local bar every Sunday night to answer some of these questions and many came, including bikers, musicians and those on the fringes of society – the vast majority of whom had very little church connection whatsoever. The gatherings aimed to provide opportunity for expression of and enquiry into the Christian faith in a relaxed pub environment. The format consisted of quality live music and other performance art and straight talking in languages and images that relate at street level.

Over the next seven years, somewhere in the region of 300 events took place, using dozens of musicians, storytellers and artists, and a significant number of people benefited from the community that surrounded them. Some folk were encouraged in their recovery from addictions, working alongside local and national agencies. Others, whose faith had been battered by negative church experience, had their wounds tended. Still more found a level of communication they could relate and respond to, to see their Christian faith develop. Some people have stuck around, for many it was an important staging post, others were travellers passing through.

Zac's Place now continues to meet in its own venue in The Gospel Hall in George Street, Swansea. As people have grown and matured in their walk following Jesus, this community of

---

faith has emerged into being a church – a church for raga-muffins. The venue is used by different groups throughout the week including offering a daily breakfast for the street home-less, a weekly Bible study and an evening soup kitchen.

New disciples are being formed and more experienced disci-ples are being renewed.[35]

The need to make disciples is nothing new. Although the transitive use of μαθετής (make disciples) is peculiar to the New Testament and occurs only three times (Matt. 13.52 and 28.19–20; Acts 14.21), one of these has had an enormous impact on Christian mission: the words of Jesus known as the Great Commission.

> Go therefore and make disciples of all nations, baptizing them in the name of the Father and of the Son and of the Holy Spirit, and teaching them to obey everything that I have commanded you. (Matt. 28.19–20)

Commenting on this verse, Steven Croft suggests that 'If ever a single verse could be said to have shaped the history of the world, this is the one. We should be careful as we weigh it and interpret it for today.'[37]

Fresh expressions are one contemporary response to this age-less imperative. One of the ways in which, in time, it will be right to examine the fruitfulness of this movement of mission will be to determine how many new disciples have been formed and how deep that discipleship is. The General Secretary of the Brit-ish Methodist Church, Martyn Atkins, believes that the signs are encouraging, saying of fresh expressions: 'I find discipleship

---

36 Adapted from www.freshexpressions.org.uk/stories/zacsplace with kind per-mission.

37 S. Croft, 'Jesus the Evangelist (According to Matthew)', address to the Fellow-ship of Parish Evangelists, January 2007.

almost happens at an accelerated pace.'[38] In the next chapter we will consider how disciples are being formed.

And as they are formed, a new wave of leaders, lay and ordained, is emerging. These leaders share many things in common with those in other forms of ministry. They need to be people of call and character. They need to be relational people honouring their relationships with God, their family and friends, their fellow leaders, those who have authority over them and those they serve. They need to be collaborative and enabling in their leadership and also courageous in their decision-making. Graham Cray argues that what leaders in fresh expressions are most tasked with is discernment: 'If Christian mission is about "Seeing what God is doing and joining in" . . . then discernment, and the cultivating of an environment which enables discernment, are the leadership capacities most needed at this time.'[39]

In Chapter 1 we noted the crucial role of the Holy Spirit in the formation and growth of the first expressions. Drawing on Acts, which documents both the role of the Spirit and the role of the apostles, Joanne Cox highlights characteristics of Spirit-inspired leadership that were vital in the planting of the very first Christian churches, characteristics that are key to healthy leadership in fresh expressions today:

Leadership is about noticing and discerning potential. It is about being a person of recognizable character (Acts 9.23–30). Leadership is about spending time mentoring other people. This can take a long time (11.25–30). Leadership is about being chosen, commissioned and prayerfully set aside for a task by a bigger group of people (12.25—13.3). Leadership is about stepping up at the opportune moment. It is also about letting the succession continue, and stepping back at the opportune moment (13.4–12). Leadership is about using your experience and background, as well as knowing the context to which you

38 M. Atkins, talking on *Expressions: The DVD* 2, Chapter 9, London: Church House Publishing 2007.

39 G. Cray, *The Discerning Leader: Co-operating with the Go-between God*, Cambridge: Grove Books, 2010, p. 7.

are speaking (13.16–45). Leadership comes with persecution: the challenge is to stay on track (13.46–52). Leadership is about knowing when to leave and when to stay (14.1–7). Leadership is about pointing to something greater (14.8–18). Leadership is not a bed of roses. Sometimes it is about being hurt and knowing that there are other people who will gather around and walk back to the 'city' with you (14.19–20). Leadership is about being accountable and testifying honestly to what God is doing (14.26–8). Leadership is about asking tough theological questions and wrestling with the answers in the midst of those wiser and more discerning (15.1–21). Leadership is about discerning the right team at the right time (15.22–35). Leadership comes with conflict. Succession is a mark of success (15.36–41).[40]

Although the fresh expressions movement is comparatively young, the issue of leadership succession is already prominent, along with the concomitant need to raise up new indigenous leadership. Where there is a healthy culture of discipleship a natural fruit of that culture will be the production of new leadership. Ruth Poch tells how new leaders are being formed at re:generation, a fresh expression that was born as a youth church but is becoming all-age:

A core value of the work of re:generation has been discipleship. Now weekly Bible studies are increasingly led by the young people, and they also have rotas to lead the prayer ministry time and input from Scripture. Our discipleship groups for guys and girls are peer led so that's very much about going deeper and being able to share things in a safe environment. To have that more intimate setting and the prayer support that comes from that have been key factors in establishing those groups.

At the beginning we prayed for more adult volunteers, but it never seemed that God really answered that prayer. In hindsight it has been a blessing, because we had to use the young people in the work of the church, or take risks with them serving in

40 Adapted from the *Mission-Shaped Ministry* course unit, 'Leadership Matters', with kind permission.

ways that we wouldn't have done had we had more mature people coming along at that stage.[41]

As well as forming individual disciples and new leaders, fresh expressions are very conscious of the need to form community. Talking about her experiences at Moot in London, one member explains that 'for me it is very important that there is a community'.[42] Within two genres of fresh expressions, community is particularly prominent. The first is the new monastic genre that is proving to be particularly fruitful with young adults.[43] New monastic communities place a very high value on hospitality and welcome – the meal table and the breaking of bread are often central – and are characterized by shared rules of life, rhythms of prayer and cycles of biblical reading.

The other genre is church planting in new residential areas. At The Beacon in Dartford, pioneer minister Bart Woodhouse has been dubbed 'Mr Community' by the residents on the new housing estate where he lives with his family. He has also been approached by Kent County Council to work for one and a half days a week as a community development worker. Blogging about this, Bart said:

> This is a real affirmation to us and will enable us to further the work we feel is so important on this new site, helping it become a strong and vibrant community. It also affirms our position in the new community as a church, and helps us communicate that the Christian life is not just sermons and worship songs, but more about changing lives and communities for the better, which is what Jesus' life and teaching is all about![44]

Meanwhile, in Loughborough, Reside was born of Anglican and Methodist parentage with the aims of contributing to community

---

41 Adapted from www.freshexpressions.org.uk/stories/regeneration, with kind permission.

42 As featured on *Expressions: The DVD 2.*

43 See G. Cray, I. Mobsby and A. Kennedy (eds), *New Monasticism as Fresh Expression of Church*, Norwich: Canterbury Press, 2010.

44 www.the-beacon.org/uncategorized/community-is-the-heart-of-mission.

and enabling residents to be actively engaged in developing the community of which they are part. Pioneer Ellie Griffin says:

> Reside cares about every aspect of community life and the individual lives of the residents who make up this community. This comes from our belief that God cares about every aspect of lives too and that the Christian faith has something to offer in each situation. So we hope that together we can develop this community into a place to which people feel they belong, were they can feel safe, respected and valued. A place where people know each other and support one another. A place people can be proud to call their community.[45]

Like all other churches, fresh expressions are also called to be transformational – collectively through the Church gathered, serving and bearing prophetic witness in its context, and through the Church dispersed, being salt and light, living out whole-life discipleship and engaging in personal mission. The former is being seen in a whole range of ways, from litter picks to Street Pastors to drug rehabilitation schemes. In the needy Redhouse area of Walsall there was very little provision for the children and families who lived on the estate. Even the local primary school closed. The local Anglican and Methodist churches came together to engage with the community and developed The Hothouse to help provide community facilities in the heart of the Redhouse area, and to share the good news of the gospel. The old hardware shop had been empty for some time. The Wednesday evening club, held at the local primary school for primary-aged children, had been running for several years and was very popular. The Hothouse began with a reviving of the club and a summer holiday club. As the work grew, so the fruits of it were seen, and a major local business joined with the churches to provide the funds to transform the former hardware shop into a permanent Christian venue where people of all ages could come and meet, belong and discover the love of Jesus. It transformed the neighbourhood.[46]

---

45 reside.org.uk/?page_id=47.

46 www.freshexpressions.org.uk/stories/hothouse.

The body of Christ spends more time scattered than gathered. Andrew Davison and Alison Milbank helpfully point out that:

> What tends to get forgotten . . . is the priesthood of the laity in the secular world: their specific mission is forgotten and under-resourced. If our mission as the Church is to unveil and reveal the Divine ordering of the world and the true humanity, then that is the task of the laity to do this wherever they live and work.[47]

Speaking on *Expressions: The DVD 2*, Steven Croft suggested that the pattern of discipleship that is emerging in fresh expressions is one of whole-life discipleship enabling Christians to be effective in Christian lifestyle and witness in the home, work and leisure contexts where they spend most of their time. To further this it will be essential that fresh expressions develop rhythms of life and patterns of worship and teaching that really do honour and support the lives people lead and the work they do, seeing these contexts as places of transformational mission and avoiding the age-old temptation to see mission only as the things that the Church does corporately.

## Ecclesial

In an address to the General Synod of the Church of England, Rowan Williams declared that through fresh expressions: 'We're rediscovering something about what the Church is.'[48] Fresh expressions of Church (to use their full title) are intended to become precisely that: new churches. They are not intended to be some form of halfway house or stepping stone en route to another church but to become mature expressions of Church themselves in due time – mature expressions shaped by the gospel and the enduring marks of the Church.

---

47  A. Davison and A. Milbank, *For the Parish: A Critique of Fresh Expressions*, London: SCM Press, 2010, p. 134.

48  Rowan Williams, 'Fresh Expressions: The Life Blood of Who we Are', address to General Synod, 28 February 2007.

In any church shaped by the gospel, most Christian traditions would expect to see a healthy ministry of word and sacrament, a community of people growing in discipleship and a missional life expressed both corporately and individually, all dedicated and nurtured through worship offered in spirit and truth. As for the enduring marks of the Church, there are different ways of understanding these, as we explored in Chapter 1. Prominent is the classical creedal understanding that the Church is called to be one, holy, catholic and apostolic, a form of being that reflects the nature of God, who is three yet one, holy, for all and sent. The Fresh Expressions team talks about the essence of Church being four relationships: an upward relationship with God (expressed in worship and holy living); an outward relationship with the world (expressed in mission); an inward relationship (expressed in community or fellowship); and an 'of' relationship (expressed through connection with the rest of the body of Christ).

The emergence of the fresh expressions movement has led to a renewed and healthy consideration of the basic question: 'What is Church?' The questions 'Is this Church?', or 'In what ways is this Church?' are rightly being asked of fresh expressions. This process has widened to a healthy reflection upon the fullness of Church experienced in more established expressions too. For many, especially the emerging generations who have little or no denominational loyalty, the question 'What is Church?' is one of essence. In his 2007 General Synod address, Rowan Williams went on to say that through fresh expressions:

> We're . . . rediscovering, to use a favourite metaphor of mine, that the Church is something that happens before it's something that is institutionally organised. It happens when the Good News summons, assembles, people around Jesus Christ. Remember that that is what we're thinking of, not a series of scattered experiments, not a series of enterprises in religious entertainment, not, God forbid, a kind of dumbing-down of the historic faith and its requirements so that more people may get vaguely interested.

The point of Fresh Expressions is the point of the Church

itself; that is to provide a place where Christ is set free in our midst.[49]

As so often, the Archbishop's thinking takes us to the very heart of the matter. The root meaning of *ecclesia* is gathering or assembly. For Archbishop Rowan, the Church is a gathering of people around the risen Jesus. It is always relational before it is institutional. Christ is firmly at the centre. Here is an understanding that is both simple and profound. It strips away the accoutrements of denominational clutter, taking us to a place where all Christians can meet and converse. It divests the Church of institutional plant and machinery that can so often be stumbling blocks to those seeking Christ. And then it invites the questions of discipleship. Who is this Jesus? How do we respond to what we have found? What is our calling as we gather and scatter? How can we share what we have found? What does this mean for the world of which we are part? To answer these questions, those gathering will need to explore both the Bible and the traditions of the Church while constantly asking what the God who says 'behold I make all things new' (Rev. 21.5 AV) is wanting to do now. If Tom Stuckey is right, and 'God is reshaping his Church',[50] fresh expressions will have an important part to play in answering the question: 'What is Church?' As we head into a post-denominational age or perhaps a truly ecumenical age, these are exciting times for the Church.

Amid this fluidity and excitement there are both further questions and challenges. What does maturity look like? Who decides when a gathering of Christians is a church? How does the wider world see things? When the Church is more open to possibilities, throwing off the shackles of Christendom, the secular authorities are increasingly looking for 'legitimate' religious communities in the light of both tighter charity regulation and the abuse of faith by those who have committed atrocities. In Howden Clough the local council initially took a dim view of the redevelopment of the

---

49 Williams, 'Fresh Expressions'.
50 T. Stuckey, 'God who inspires'.

chapel building into the Wesley Playhouse.[51] The complaint was that the church had not obtained change-of-use permission for its building. Supported by the community the church argued in the council chambers that it did not need change-of-use permission for it was still a church – an interesting exploration of ecclesiology – and duly won its case. It is not just within the wider church family but also in the wider world that fresh expressions need to be recognized as Church: truly good people and places that contribute to the wellbeing of the communities of which they are part.

## What fresh expressions are not

The mission-shaped/fresh expressions movement has released a wave of imagination and creativity across the churches. There has been a sea change in how Church is seen at both grass roots and senior leadership level. At his District Synod in September 2008, John Howard, the Chair of the Wolverhampton and Shrewsbury Methodist District, offered a prayer that the churches of the District be mission-shaped, for unless they were they would not be Church at all. Recognizing the urgency of the missiological situation, the mood music has changed. There is a new language of pioneering and risk. Most importantly there are new church communities, making new disciples and a change for good in the world in which they are set. Christian disciples are being encouraged, enabled and equipped to take steps of faith and develop fresh ways of being Church. Is this the edge of a new Pentecost, as Tom Stuckey would suggest?[52] One of the striking features of the first Christian missionaries was that they were seen to be ordinary people who did extraordinary things because they had been with Jesus (Acts 4.13). One of the remarkable features of the fresh expressions movement is how ordinary people who gather around the risen Jesus are doing extraordinary things in places many would never have heard of, such as Annan and Howden Clough.

---

51 The story of Wesley's Playhouse can be found on the Fresh Expressions DVD *Expressions: Making a Difference*.

52 Tom Stuckey, *On the Edge of Pentecost*, Peterborough: Inspire, 2007.

Even those most critical of the movement acknowledge its scale and impact. Davison and Milbank, for example, describe MSC and the subsequent encouragement of fresh expressions as 'the most significant development in the Church of England in recent years'.[53] Amid all this excitement we need to beware of a number of risks.

A first risk is exaggeration. Speaking at a Fresh Expressions vision day in Gloucestershire, the Bishop of Gloucester, Michael Perham, fresh from some sabbatical study, highlighted three things he saw happening as result of the mission-shaped/fresh expressions movement:

1 Existing churches being reshaped for mission.
2 Existing churches starting fresh expressions as an extension of their missiological life.
3 New fresh expressions being planted in places and contexts that existing churches were not connecting with.

These are all good things, but to claim they are all fresh expressions primarily for the benefit of those who are not yet members of any church would be an exaggeration. In the early days of the fresh expressions movement there were suggestions that some existing church activities were being rebranded as fresh expressions either for the kudos this brought or as a way of finding funding. True fresh expressions are not an exercise in rebranding.

A second risk is that fresh expressions become church lite. In an age when café church is cool, we need to beware of fresh expressions being all froth and no substance. The challenges of developing deep discipleship, transforming mission and holy contextual worship are significant. The stories in this chapter and those in the next show how fresh expressions take these challenges very seriously and are seeking creative and fitting ways to develop new ecclesial communities that do grow mature disciples, change the world around for good and all for the glory of God. True fresh expressions are not church lite.

---

53 Davison and Milbank, *For the Parish*, p. vii.

A third risk is that fresh expressions are seen as a bridge to or recruiting vehicles for existing congregations. One of the most painful things for those developing fresh expressions to hear is people saying, 'What you are doing is wonderful, but when are we going to see these people in church?', by which the questioner means 11 a.m. on a Sunday morning or whenever it is their church gathers for worship. Church is Church whenever and wherever people gather around the risen Jesus – it is also Church when scattered as salt and light in the everyday contexts of work, leisure and personal relationships. Fresh expressions are not halfway houses to 'proper' Church. They are valid and valued parts of the Church catholic.

A fourth risk is that fresh expressions are viewed provisionally. The development of fresh expressions was initially placed in the Projects, Research and Development cluster of the national Methodist team structure. Did this imply that fresh expressions are not quite seen as being real Church yet? Significantly perhaps it now resides with Discipleship and Ministries. Similarly, in a lot of the literature fresh expressions are often referred to as projects. This provisional language is not helpful. We don't see babies or young children as projects of humanity but rather human beings in themselves, albeit ones with much learning and developing to do. One archdeacon described fresh expressions as the R&D department of the Diocese. In one way this is understandable but it retains the dangers of provisionality. When organizations, including the Church, face tough challenges with resources, they often cut the R&D departments! To return to Rowan Williams, fresh expressions are not 'a series of scattered experiments'.[54] They are emerging churches.

A fifth and final risk is the one famously cited by John Hull, that in an age when we are looking for a mission-shaped Church we actually end up with a Church-shaped mission.[55] This risk will be realized if we forget two things. First of all that the responsibility for building the Church is actually Jesus' not ours. As Martyn

---

54 Williams, 'Fresh Expression'.

55 J. Hull, *Mission-Shaped Church: A Theological Response*, London: SCM Press, 2006.

Atkins is fond of pointing out, Jesus says 'I will build my Church', you 'Go and make disciples'. The second thing we forget at our peril is that the horizon we are aiming for is not the Church but the kingdom, as we are reminded every time we pray the Lord's Prayer. Fresh expressions are called to be communities, signs and foretastes of the kingdom.

The risks explored here are real. The good news illustrated in the stories of this chapter and explored in the principles of the next is that there are an increasing number of newly forming churches that understand themselves to be called into being and shaped by God the Father, gathered around and honouring God the Son and guided by God the Spirit to participate in the divine mission and to see the kingdom come in the lives of individuals communities and the wider world.

## Further reading and resources

Atkins, M., *Discipleship . . . and the People Called Methodists*, Peterborough: Methodist Church, 2010.

Church of England Mission and Public Affairs Council, *Mission-Shaped Church*, 2nd edn, London: Church House Publishing, 2009.

Clark, D. (ed.), *Reshaping the Mission of Methodism*, Aberystwyth: Church in the Market Place Publications, 2011.

Cray, G., *The Discerning Leader: Co-operating with the Go-between God*, Cambridge: Grove Books, 2010.

Cray, G., Mobsby, I. and Kennedy, A., *New Monasticism as Fresh Expression of Church*, Norwich: Canterbury Press, 2010.

Croft, S. (ed.), *The Future of the Parish System: Shaping the Church of England for the 21st Century*, London: Church House Publishing, 2006.

Croft, S., 'Jesus the Evangelist (According to Matthew)', Address to the Fellowship of Parish Evangelists, January 2007.

Croft, S. and Mobsby, I. (eds), *Fresh Expressions in the Sacramental Tradition*, Norwich: Canterbury Press, 2009.

Davison, A. and Milbank, A., *For the Parish: A Critique of Fresh Expressions*, London: SCM Press, 2010.

Drane, J. and Fleming-Drane, O., 'Reformed, Reforming, Emerging and Experimenting: A Study in Contextual Theology Reflecting the Experiences of Initiatives in Emerging Ministry being Funded by the Church of Scotland', Church of Scotland Ministries Council and the Mission and Discipleship Council, 2010.

Dunn, J., *The Acts of the Apostles*, Peterborough: Epworth Press, 1996.

Hull, J., *Mission-Shaped Church: A Theological Response*, London: SCM Press, 2006.

Jackson, B., *Hope for the Church*, London: Church House Publishing, 2002, p. 132.

Lings, G., 'A Golden Opportunity', *Encounters on the Edge* 50, 2011.

Methodist Church, *Over to You 2004: Reports from the Methodist Conference*, Peterborough: Methodist Publishing House, 2004.

Nelstrop, L. and Percy, M., *Evaluating Fresh Expressions*, Norwich: Canterbury Press, 2008.

Pillinger, P. and Roberts, A., *Changing Church for a Changing World*, Peterborough: Methodist Publishing House, 2007.

Roberts, A., 'The Acts of the Apostles: Resourcing and Developing Fresh Expressions of Church', *Epworth Review* 36.3, 2009.

Shier-Jones, A., *Pioneer Ministry and Fresh Expressions of Church*, London: SPCK, 2009.

Smith, A., *God-Shaped mission*, Norwich: Canterbury Press, 2008.

Stuckey, T., *On the Edge of Pentecost*, Peterborough: Inspire, 2007.

Williams, R., 'Fresh Expressions: The Life Blood of Who we Are', address to General Synod. 28th February 2007.

## DVDs

Fresh Expressions: *Expressions: The DVD*
Fresh Expressions: *Expression: The DVD 2*
Fresh Expressions: *Sanctus*
Fresh Expressions: *Expressions: Making a Difference*

## Websites

www.freshexpressions.org.uk
www.freshexpressions.ca
www.safespace.me.uk
www.sharetheguide.org
www.tubestation.org

# 4

# Best Practice in Fresh Expressions

## How healthy fresh expressions develop

As fresh expressions form in a great variety of contexts and out of a great range of traditions, a body of wisdom and a growing literature – both web-based and printed – is emerging about how healthy fresh expressions develop. There is also a growing awareness of the pitfalls and problems that can arise as people seek to grow new forms of Church, and much can be learnt from this as well. In this chapter we shall explore some of the principles behind healthy fresh expressions and consider some of the things that can hinder fruitful development.

### In the beginning: God

In Chapter 1 we explored the nature of God as Trinity and as pioneer. In Chapter 3 we suggested that the vital first question for a group of Christians considering forming a fresh expression is the simple and yet so complex question: 'What is God like?' If fresh expressions are to develop healthily, this thinking is vital. The four words from the very beginning of the Bible are foundational for Christian thinking about any subject, including fresh expressions of Church. They remind us that God is the source and origin of all that is. In *God-Shaped Mission*, Alan Smith comments: 'The danger with our current preoccupation to make the Church 'mission-shaped' is that we might take our eyes off God and shift our focus to ourselves or to the Church.' He goes on to critique the theology of mission within *Mission-Shaped Church* (MSC), arguing that: 'The report develops a theology of mission by concentrating not on the 'being' of God as Trinity, but on the 'action' of God in creation and redemption.' The word 'concentrating' is important here as to be fair to MSC it does make several references to God as Trinity, drawing in particular on this way of being in conversations about unity and diversity and the nature and activity of God in creation and redemption. Having stressed his keenness to support 'any attempt to help the Church become more mission-shaped', Smith goes on to say that 'the essential starting point is not mission, but God himself'.[1]

If fresh expressions are signs of God at work then these newly forming Christian communities should reflect, embody and make known the character of the God at work in them. How fresh expressions answer the question 'What is God like?' will have a profound effect on the form of Church that emerges.

If God is creative – the first thing we learn about God in the Bible – then our churches should be creative. If God is life-giving, our churches should be life-giving. If God is holy and just then our churches should be marked by holiness and justice. If, supremely, God is love then it follows that our churches should be characterized by love above all else. Thankfully we know God to be gracious and merciful, so these should be characteristics of our churches too, especially when we don't always agree with each other.

Healthy fresh expressions are God-centred communities. To stay close to the heart of God, the planting community will faithfully partake of the regular Christian disciplines of prayer, worship and the breaking of bread. They will seek to model their life on the Trinity, recognize God's presence within the people they encounter and carefully seek God's guidance for all that they do.

---

To stay close to the heart of God, Wolverhampton Pioneer Ministries are developing 'rhythms of grace', daily patterns of shared prayer and Bible study together with shared meals and regular Eucharists. Worship and fellowship are important in themselves but also shape the community for mission.

---

1 A. Smith, *God-Shaped Mission*, Norwich: Canterbury Press, 2008, pp. 50–2.

For those seeking to evaluate fresh expressions (or any form of Church for that matter), the most important question will be: 'How fully does this community reflect the nature of God?'

## Culturally authentic

The Fresh Expressions team's definition states that a fresh expression will be shaped for its cultural context. Healthy fresh expressions will know their place well, whether that place be geographic or a network of relationships. Part of this knowing will involve having a developed theology of place. John Inge, in *A Christian Theology of Place*, draws an important distinction between spaces and places. In Inge's view spaces are empty husks devoid of character or meaning, whereas places are areas known, owned and filled with meaning and value. For those planting fresh expressions it is essential to understand the values and meanings held in a particular place, to reflect on the activity of God and signs of the kingdom already present, to be wise in discerning anything that may be hostile to the grace of God – before seeking to make the gospel known in new ways.

In her very helpful book, *The Word in Place*, Louise Lawrence explores how the word can again be made flesh in a variety of places, especially through contextually fitting ways of reading the New Testament and what she describes as a 'hermeneutic of presence'[2] that centres on the interpretation of scripture that comes from reading it alongside others in a particular place.

There are at least three types of place in which Christians may be called to plant a fresh expression, and the thinking about place encouraged by Inge and Lawrence is helpful for all of them.

## A familiar place

Much is rightly made of the need for cross-cultural missionaries in twenty-first-century Britain, and we will consider this shortly. But with a majority of the population having no conscious and mean-

---

2 L. Lawrence, *The Word in Place*, London: SPCK, 2009.

ingful relationship with Christ, there are thousands of people within the regular orbit of disciples of Jesus who need to be introduced to him. There is an urgent need for Christians – especially younger Christians – to be able to form Church within cultures and contexts that are familiar to them.

Some may want to argue that this is precisely the missionary task of existing churches: to serve their immediate context. In support of this argument there are many excellent examples of churches of all denominations and traditions doing precisely this, and indeed the renewed emphasis on mission following MSC has led many Christians and churches to reconnect with the *missio Dei* in their area. Mission action planning is enjoying a renaissance. Many of those doing the Fresh Expressions course called Mission-Shaped Ministry are people from existing churches who want to see them become more mission-shaped. Many fresh expressions are forming on the fringes of these churches, in particular Messy Churches and café churches that meet on church premises. All sorts of creative and costly missional initiatives are being developed, especially among children and young people. Following the publication of *Mission-Shaped Parish*[3] in 2006, a growing library of literature has emerged championing the missionary role of the inherited Church. This is all good and to be encouraged.

As ever there is a 'but'. In many places, as the years have gone by, a large cultural gap has emerged between many churches and the very communities in which they are set. In these places, if the church will not change then, for the sake of the gospel and the community, something new will be needed – preferably owned, blessed and backed by the existing churches. New wine in new wineskins (Matt. 9.17).

In a small town in the West Midlands, a parish church had a large DayGlow poster advertising an evening of inspirational choral music. On the other side of the road, directly opposite the notice board, there was a small row of shops with a bookmaker, tattoo shop and chippy lined up adjacently. The road was wide

---

3 P. Bayes, T. Sledge, J. Holbrook, M. Rylands and M. Seeley, *Mission-Shaped Parish: Traditional Church in a Changing World*, London: Church House Publishing, 2006.

but the cultural gap between the two sides was enormous. Why would anyone placing a tenner on Wayne Rooney to score first, before adding a tattoo to their collection and ending their afternoon with a bag of battered chips,[4] cross the road to imbibe the works of John Rutter?

There were very few if any tattoos evident among the concert clientele as they arrived in their well-polished cars. As I surveyed the scene, the irony struck me that the church was not so much for the parish as for a network of those who enjoy a particular style of music, art and probably liturgy. To its credit the church was still there. Just around the corner from the chippy, the former local Methodist church was closed. I wondered what John Wesley would have made of the scene? Do his 'four alls' still have something to say? All need to be saved, all can be saved, all can know they are saved and all can be saved to the uttermost. My mind went to Romans 10.14: 'How, then, can they call on the one they have not believed in? And how can they believe in the one of whom they have not heard?' (NIV).

Methodism was so effective as a missionary movement in its infancy, saving thousands of souls and possibly the nation from self destruction, because it raised up a small army of people who could speak the languages of the gospel and the ordinary person in the local culture. It raised up indigenous leadership. If the fresh expressions movement is truly to change the landscape,[5] then a great number of new indigenous leaders will need to be raised up or released.

In the Kent coastal town of Deal the parish church of St George's had a nice problem. The congregation had grown to the point where it was too big for the building that itself was the largest building in the town. Sheila Porter takes up the story:

---

4 Yes – they really do sell battered chips.

5 At the time of writing, the Fresh Expressions team has presented two national conferences entitled *Changing the Landscape*.

The challenge for us in 2002 was: How are we going to shape a Church that can keep on growing? That wasn't dependent on the size of the building, wasn't dependent upon the number of professional leaders. We had a church that was full but, beyond that – well, we wanted to create a church that could engage with today's culture and particularly for those who would not step over the threshold of a church building. We wanted to get out there and see the kingdom built outside of church buildings.

So now we have missional communities and these are communities of people whose focus is on mission. They have a particular mission task, a network that they are focusing on in terms of mission and they can be generally anything from 15 up to 60 people, and these missional communities are sometimes called clusters.

It's like a whole treasure trove has been opened, and people who previously were sitting in the pews are now doing all kinds of things that they never dreamed they would be doing. As they've gone out and taken on these new roles, new responsibilities, got involved, rolled up their sleeves in these things, they've discovered the need to depend upon God, and so they've grown spiritually and in their discipleship as well and, of course from it, one of the big things has been the whole release of leaders, and again these people were sitting in the pews before but now we have 40 missional leaders who are out there leading, and that has been fantastic.[6]

One of the keys to the effectiveness of these new leaders is that they already know and are part of the culture they are seeking to serve and plant a fresh expression in. Reflecting on the final of the BBC programme *Apprentice 2011* in which candidates had been scrutinized on the basis of their business plans, Lord Alan

---

6 Taken from the Fresh Expressions DVD *Expressions: Making a Difference*, with permission.

Sugar commented on how most successful entrepreneurs develop their businesses in fields that are familiar to them – cultures and contexts where they have both experience and credibility. There is transferable learning here for fresh expressions. Pioneering ministries/fresh expressions are likely to develop most quickly in contexts and cultures familiar to the pioneer(s).

The Tubestation[7] church for surfers in Cornwall – supported by the Methodist Church – has been one of the most feted and inspiring stories to emerge from the fresh expressions movement. The leaders, Henry Cavender and Kris Lannen, with characteristic humility centre all they do on God the Trinity: 'the ultimate ride can only be found in Jesus'. Henry explains: 'These [the surfers] are people who are immersed in the wonder of creation. Our job is to point out where they're already experiencing God.'[8] This is key to their effectiveness and so too is their credibility in their context. Both keen surfers, Henry and Kris speak the language, look the part and instinctively know what makes those they serve tick.

> Surfers tend to be searchers. They travel the world looking for the ultimate ride, a tube, where the wave bowls over your head. It's the most coveted surfing experience, and has been described as a religious experience. Everything slows down, sound changes, it's an amazing thing.[9]

## A cross-cultural place

If fresh expressions are truly to be an outworking of the Great Commission to go and make disciples among all people groups, then there will need to be ever more cross-cultural missionaries who can go beyond cultures and contexts familiar to them. In particular those who can go the highways and byways and help form Christian community among the most vulnerable in society – the poor, the crippled, the lame and the blind of Luke 14.13. We

7 www.tubestation.org.
8 www.freshexpressions.org.uk/node/510.
9 www.freshexpressions.org.uk/node/510.

need fresh expressions with dirty fingernails as well as cool cappuccinos. Fresh expressions that connect with people like 'Sam' who is part of Grafted, a Church Army-led fresh expression in the Scottish borders:

> Life before I met Paul and Elaine Little who run the Grafted project was pretty shocking to be honest. When I was 13 years old, I started smoking cannabis, and by the time I was 14, I had started to become a dealer selling quite large amounts for my age at the time and really the draw of money and power and respect was very high, and I very quickly became addicted, and I gradually worked my way up the ladder and started taking harder drugs.
>
> Eventually when I was 19, I ended up with a really bad cocaine habit, and I had a heart attack at the age of 20 induced by an overdose and then shortly after that I started taking heroin – I was addicted to heroin for about a year and I was put on methadone for two years. To be honest it really wasn't much of what I'd call a life, it wasn't really living. I got to the stage where I think that God brought me to such a level where I had no option but to cry out to him and ask for his forgiveness, and being with Paul and Elaine and the rest of the people on the project, they actually helped me through my withdrawals when I decided to come off methadone. They prayed me through it and I do know for a fact that it was nowhere near as bad as what it should have been. That was the power of God working in my life to help me through that struggle.[10]

Getting to know and be known and trusted by these places and cultures, and the people who are part of them, is often a long, challenging and draining process. As Angela Shier-Jones put it: 'Pioneering ministry cannot be done to a community by someone who knows what they need, it can only be done with a community by someone who shares their need.'[11]

---

10 *Expressions: Making a Difference.*

11 A. Shier-Jones, *Pioneer Ministry and Fresh Expressions of Church*, London: SPCK, 2009, p. 123.

In sharing the story of the development of Somewhere Else in Liverpool, Barbara Glasson tells of how she spent a whole year walking the streets to get to know her place.[12] For Jim and Juliet Kilpin one of the biggest challenges in forming Cable Street Community Church in Shadwell lay in convincing the community that they were not going to disappear like many others who had come into the area with the honest intent of trying to help the community. In communities where relationships are often transient and short-term, pioneers who stay and go deep will model something of the faithfulness, steadfastness and dependability of God.[13] This is a costly and sacrificial calling in a broken and fragile world.

As I write this, the streets of Britain are aflame with riots. The blame game is beginning. Could this be a time when God is calling for fresh expressions to be good news among the brokenness? Rallied by this message on Facebook – 'Come with broom, bin bags, gloves and cleaning equip. It's not about the cleaning. It's about loving the city'[14] – the young adults of Wolverhampton Pioneer Ministries (WPM) marched with their brooms alongside other people of goodwill in the city as they declared peace in place of strife the morning after a night of rioting and looting. Arun Arora, the leader of WPM, was prominent among community leaders calling for an end to the violence and for peace to prevail. The members of this city-centre fresh expression were visibly living out this prayerful song of Jodi Page-Clark.

> LOOK AROUND YOU, can you see?
> Times are troubled, people grieve.
> See the violence, feel the hardness;
> All my people, weep with me.
>
> *Kyrie eleison, Christe eleison,*
> *Kyrie eleison.*

---

12 Fresh Expressions, *Expressions: The DVD.*
13 Fresh Expressions, *Expressions: The DVD.*
14 www.facebook.com/pages/Wolverhampton-Pioneer-Ministries.

Walk among them, I'll go with you.
Reach out to them with my hands.
Suffer with me, and together
We will serve them, help them stand.

Forgive us Father; hear our prayer.
We would walk with you anywhere,
Through your suffering, with forgiveness,
Take your life into the land.

## New places

A growing number of fresh expressions are being planted in territory wholly untouched by the Church, especially new housing estates – places where there is little or no formed sense of culture, context or community. One such place is the Glasgow Harbour Development. Pioneer minister Alex Smeed shares how he and his team have sought to understand their missional context.

We undertook an 18-month-long mission audit in order to understand the culture of – not only the people – but what the buildings say, and what the cars people drive say about them. What the shops that are built around about, what do they say about the type of people that live in Glasgow Harbour? Our focus in the mission audit was really on two aspects. There was qualitative data, which is really about the impressions that you build up, so the way that we did that was to look at the websites; look at the websites of the developers – trying to understand who they were selling these flats to. It was about hanging around actually on the streets and on the promenade – trying to just understand who the people were, what the kind of culture they came from was like, what hours they kept, where they worked, and all of that was about getting to know people. So the other aspect of it was the quantitative analysis – that was a much more book-based type of analysis where we'd end up in the Mitchell Library in Glasgow, and we'd be looking at the old Ordnance Survey maps of the area – looking at the history books – seeing who used to own this land and understanding all the different aspects of what it means to be part of this area and how it was built upon for centuries and see where we could go in the future – the kind of keys to the gospel – the ways in which we could understand things to be moving in the future.[15]

The qualitative approach described above is observational. Alongside this the conversational is vital. As my colleague Michael Moynagh is fond of saying: 'If you want to know what those you are seeking to share with need or think, *ask* them!'

In virgin territory there is a particular need for fresh expressions to be formers of community in the widest sense of that word. With property developers exploiting planning regulations to build the maximum number of dwellings and the lowest amount of community space, this is quite a challenge. In Glasgow Harbour the only communal spaces are the foyers and lifts in the apartment blocks and the car parks and petrol station outside.

In *The Word in Place*, Louise Lawrence quotes eight principles suggested by Michael Langrish for how churches should model true community. They are pertinent for fresh expressions being birthed in new areas. The church Langrish suggests needs to be:

- incarnational and embodied – physically involved in, attending to and being with the immediate community
- a unifying force bringing people together
- 'fuzzy edged', 'open doored' and welcoming
- celebratory at the heart of major moments in the life of the community
- light on structures and participatory
- open to premises being used by others (if it owns property – many fresh expression will actually live by the complement of this and use the premises of others (see for example the Lounge@Costa))[16]

---

15 *Expressions: Making a Difference.*
16 *Expressions: Making a Difference.*

- a community with a culture of nurture and growth that encourages interdependence as well as personal development
- (most importantly) rooted in the scriptures and exhibiting God's love.

The fuzzy-edged point is interesting and reflects a shift in thinking from a 'believe, belong, behave' approach to evangelism and discipleship, to a 'belong, behave, believe' approach.

In Chapter 3 we introduced the story of Reside, a Christian project evolving in response to growing housing developments to the south of Loughborough. Here Methodist Deacon Ellie Griffin illustrates how a number of Langrish's principles are being put into practice in the place Reside serves.

Our vision is to be an evolving Christian network that provides safe and welcoming places, explores the Christian faith, cares for the community and collectively expresses each element of Church.

We aim to contribute to community by enabling residents to be actively engaged in developing the area in which they live – whether that's through the residents' association, involvement with schools, Neighbourhood Watch, litter picks or working with children and young people. The opportunities really are endless and the range of skills needed is diverse.

We want to get people excited about getting to know their neighbours and to provide opportunities for building relationships. There aren't many meeting places on the estate and so we are trying to be imaginative in how we address this so that all groups within the community can interact more with each other.

So far Reside has been involved in the Haddon Way Residents' Association, working with them to listen to the community's needs or concerns and hosting Community Fun Days, a Big Tidy Up event and an outdoor Christmas carol service. We have also hosted Easter Fun Days on the Grange Park housing development two years running, giving the families opportunity to meet their neighbours and have fun together.

We are very much developing cells at the moment and we're just starting a pilot cell of people who will be leaders in different cell groups. We have got lots of good contacts now on the edges of the community but how can we take it a bit further? I think the cell church model, tweaked to this context, would be a very good model for us.[17]

## Humble

Fruitful fresh expressions and those leading them know their God, know their place and know themselves. They are humble. They know their strengths and they know their weaknesses. They have the wisdom to build on the former and to address the latter. Wise pioneers know their own limitations, where they can get help and how to build effective communities in which the gifts of everyone are celebrated and used. Above all they are clear about their call. Pioneer ministry may have an attractive cachet for some but the reality is often tough, demanding and sacrificial – but then isn't all true Christian discipleship? Tim Lea testifies to this when talking about the development of The Bridge in Hinckley: 'We have got dirty, muddy, disillusioned and fed up but I would rather stand before God . . . and say I tried than have sat and been comfortable and to have never tried in the first place.'[18] What sustains pioneers such as Tim above all else is the deep conviction that this is what God has called them to do. In Chapters 5–7 we shall explore more fully the call to pioneer ministry and how one can be sustained in this vocation.

There are some who have been at least wary, if not suspicious of and occasionally hostile to fresh expressions, criticizing them for what is perceived to be a lack of appreciation of the inherited

17 www.freshexpressions.org.uk/stories/reside, used with permission.
18 *Expressions: The DVD.*

Church. Some have suggested that inherited systems have been 'belittled and cast as unhelpful and irrelevant in Fresh Expressions writing'.[19] In any new and young movement there are bound to be irritants and sadly there are examples of nascent fresh expressions that have not properly respected other Christian churches. Having said that, in this author's experience those championing the movement, such as Rowan Williams and Martyn Atkins, the Fresh Expressions agency and its associates and the majority of fresh expressions, have been deeply committed to the Archbishops' vision for a 'mixed-economy' Church in which both inherited and new forms see themselves as partners together in the mission of God and members together of the body of Christ. While some dismiss this as 'a fig leaf',[20] Graham Cray is at pains to point out that:

> Our context requires far more than fresh expressions of Church. It requires firstly that weekly partnership, which Archbishop Rowan has called 'a mixed-economy Church'. In a mixed-economy Church, every parish church and chapel, every deanery, circuit, synod and presbytery knows that it is called to mission through word and deed – mission is the calling of both dimensions, of the mixed economy; finding ways to give local expression to the various dimensions of mission.[21]

This commitment to a mixed economy does not mean there won't be disagreements and points of tension, but from Acts 4 onwards, when has there been a time when the whole Church agreed on everything?

---

19 A. Davison and A. Milbank, *For the Parish: A Critique of Fresh Expressions*, London: SCM, 2010, p. ix.

20 Davison and Milbank, *For the Parish*, p. 75.

21 www.freshexpressions.org.uk/changingthelandscape/2011/grahamcray.

## Discipleship is the key

In Chapter 3 we explored the importance of fresh expressions being disciple-forming communities. If there is one thing above all others that will determine the value of the fresh expressions movement, it will be its contribution to the formation and nurture of new Christian disciples across the spectra of age, culture and location. According to Martyn Atkins, 'Emerging churches are challenged, because, unless they produce Christian *disciples*, they will fail at the deepest level to be true *churches* at all.'[22]

As well as being at the heart of the calling of fresh expressions and therefore an end in itself, the making of new disciples of Christ is also key to the growth and sustainability of new forms of Church. From the apostles Andrew and Philip onwards, disciples of Jesus have introduced others to him or invited others to come and see (John 1.41, 43–6). Healthy disciples make other disciples. As noted in the previous chapter, healthy disciples will be the people from whom indigenous leadership will emerge. In the Black Country, where I am based, it is striking how may of the Pentecostal churches encourage their young Christians into leadership roles. They often go on to be worship leaders and youth pastors, many becoming senior pastors in their churches. There is a really healthy culture of apprenticing disciples and leaders. This is evident in a number of fresh expressions too. Ruth and Jamie Poch have this to say about the Re:generation youth church in Romford:

> Certainly we have always put a great emphasis on them being in leadership and I think that's been very much part of what we try to do – with the discipleship very early on. I think it's really important that young adults and young people are included in the leadership team in a church like re:generation because they are able to reflect values and ideas that many young people face in the world today. If a church is looking to reach this age group it's really important that young people and young adults

---

22 M. Atkins, *Resourcing Renewal*, Peterborough: Inspire, 2007, p. 164.

are able to have a voice within the leadership team so that they are able to contribute ideas.

One of the young leaders had this say about his role:

> As part of the leadership team one of my roles is to oversee a pod-group and what that allows us to do is allow people to mix socially with people they wouldn't necessarily mix with and also allow pastoral oversight. As a pod-leader it's my job – or my role – to check up on people perhaps on a weekly basis – to see if there's anything I need to be praying for and then if there's any more serious issues that can be directed higher up into the church – for specific pastoral care.[23]

When thinking about leadership we need to beware of too church-centric a vision. While good discipleship will develop leaders within the Christian community it will also develop Christian leaders who can be kingdom agents within all parts of God's world. In an article reflecting on the focus of discipleship among young adults, Martyn Atkins commented: 'Following [Jesus] today is more about transforming the world and less about keeping the ecclesial show on the road.'[24] All expressions of Church should be equipping and supporting people for kingdom activity – I am ever mindful of the church that has a sign over the door saying the mission starts now, which people see as they are leaving. Workplaced fresh expressions could have a particular calling to raise and support a new wave of kingdom-focused Christian nurses, teachers, bankers, shop assistants and police officers being salt and light wherever God has placed them.

Healthy disciples will make other disciples. They will grow into leaders within and beyond the Christian community. And they will know how to give. David Watson used to say that the last part of a person to be converted was their wallet or their purse, which is interesting when Jesus talked about money more than any other subject. There is lot of angst among fresh expressions about financial sustainability, much of which is genuine and understandable.

---

23 *Expressions: Making a Difference.*
24 M. Atkins, 'OPPS not OOPS!', *Methodist Recorder* 8014, 28 July 2011, p. 16.

But is it always necessary? In an age of austerity, could God be calling Christians to develop simple forms of Church that don't require much financial investment? Or is the call to sacrificial giving? A couple of miles away from my home a local evangelical church planted a new congregation in a local school. Within two years 30 people were paying for a full-time pastor because of their particular theology of giving. Healthy disciples will be generous and sacrificial in their giving.

So how are healthy disciples being formed in fresh expressions? When I spoke with a dozen fresh expressions leaders, three key ingredients for making disciples became apparent:

1 The creation of a sacramental environment.
2 Supportive relationships.
3 Intentional and contextually fitting learning.

## Creating a sacramental environment

Leaders spoke of the need for a culture of openness and grace, for safe spaces in which there is honesty, room to question, try and fail. They were seeking to create communities where belonging comes before believing and that model holistic living. They spoke of the formative power of a rich spiritual life of prayer and worship and a deep sense of God's imminence and transcendence. Barbara Glasson said that at Somewhere Else in Liverpool they sought to make disciples 'through friendship, laughter, being real with each other, finding a way to engage in honest conversation, honouring questions, encouragement and mutual learning', while Ian Mobsby at Moot in London explained that 'Grace and radical generosity are the focus of the community and its understanding of the New-Testament word *ekklesia* for the Church.'

What was being described by the practitioners was a sacramental environment. Those I dialogued with are seeking to develop communities that model the grace of God. This sacramental dynamic is given practical expression through table fellowship and a culture of hospitality. In this sort of environment the making of disciples flourishes. Mary Gray-Reeves and Michael Perham explore this culture in emerging churches in Britain and the United States in their book, *The Hospitality of God*.[25] Having visited 14 fresh expressions they were both impressed by the quality of what they experienced, the care and creativity with which services were prepared and the welcoming hospitality that was offered.

Within the sacramental environment the specific sacrament of Holy Communion was highly valued by the practitioners (right across the ecclesiological spectrum). Many fresh expressions have a profound sense of the Eucharist as a place where we meet with Christ, however creatively or humbly the arrangements by which the sacrament is celebrated. Speaking of his experience at Sanctus1 in Manchester, Ben Edson said 'Communion is central to Sanctus1. It is the way that people feel part of the community, and for some has been a rite of passage into the community. It helps sustain community and focus us on the central focus of our discipleship – the person of Christ.'

The Methodist report, *Share this Feast*, affirms the importance of Holy Communion for nourishing discipleship and mission: 'The nourishment we receive is not for ourselves alone, but in order that God may empower us to go out into the world, find out what God is doing there and join in.'[26] As new mission-shaped churches form, the sacrament of Holy Communion is itself shaping new disciples and fresh missional activity. The Lord's Supper is being celebrated carefully, creatively and contextually in many newly forming churches. A growing literature tells the stories of the ways in which communities such as Blessed, Moot and the Transcendence Mass are drawing deep on the sacramental tradition of the Church and making Christ known afresh through the Eucharist shared in fresh ways.[27]

---

25 M. Gray-Reeves and M. Perham, *The Hospitality of God*, London: SPCK, 2011.

26 *Share this Feast*, The Methodist Church, 2006, p. 38.

27 For more on these stories see S. Croft and I. Mobsby (eds), *Fresh Expressions in the Sacramental Tradition*, Norwich: Canterbury Press, 2009.

## Forming supportive relationships

The second key ingredient for making disciples is supportive relationships. The need for a sacramental environment points to the importance of the life of the community as a whole as a place of fellowship. Stott argues that this κοινωνία 'is a Trinitarian experience, it is our common share in God, Father, Son and Holy Spirit. But secondly, κοινωνία expresses what we share together, what we give as well as what we receive.'[28] While recognizing this, the practitioners, without exception, stressed the importance of small groups for making and nurturing disciples. The groups had different names but shared in common the features of Acts 2.42: teaching (typically the small group is seen as the key gathering for biblical study and learning), fellowship, eating/breaking bread and prayer.

Small groups were not the only forms of relationships that practitioners highlighted as important for making disciples. There were also various forms of one-to-one relationships. Some of these took the form of mentoring or apprenticing. Greene and Cottrell argue that long before Lord Sugar began his search for an apprentice, both Jesus and Paul 'were in the business of apprentices and apprentice-makers. That's what people were, apprentices – people learning to live the way that their Master lived.' They then go on to call for an apprentice making Church 'a place where everyone helps one another move along the path towards maturity in Christ'.[29] This call is being heard in many fresh expressions.

Other one-to-one relationships are more in the form of companions, with an emphasis on support and mutual accountability. Andy Jones described the Grace Church approach: 'We try and pair up people in discipleship relationships. They typically meet once a week to read the Bible together, pray and talk about issues they face. It's usually a more mature Christian meeting with a new or not-yet Christian.' Such relationships are to the mutual benefit of both. The new Christian learns from their more mature partner

28  J. Stott, *The Message of Acts*, Leicester: InterVarsity Press, 1990, p. 83.

29  M. and T. Greene, *Imagine: Let My People Grow*, Milton Keynes, Authentic Media, 2006, pp. 7–8.

while the more mature disciple is kept fresh and challenged by their new companion.

These forms of companion-based relationships are very in keeping with postmodernity. Phenomena such as Twitter, Facebook and Myspace may border on the neurotic at times but they do have values of support and accountability underlying them. Mentoring is very much in vogue, and with the number of life coaches rapidly expanding, people with a postmodern outlook may readily embrace the concept of a discipleship coach.

For biblical, theological and cultural reasons, good supportive relationships are key in fresh expressions if disciples are to form and grow.

## Intentional and contextually fitting learning

The classic New Testament understanding of the word μαθετής is a learner or follower. All of the practitioners surveyed affirmed the importance of good intentional learning for the making of disciples. While there was commonality in seeing the importance of intentional learning, there was a marked variety in approaches – another postmodern characteristic. Three groupings emerged.

The first group were happy to use externally produced teaching/learning materials. A second group have developed their own learning resources, wanting to develop learning that is incarnational and contextualized. These resources typically embrace a variety of learning styles, especially kinaesthetic, and make use of popular culture as a learning medium.

Michael Moynagh believes that we are seeing some significant movements in approaches to teaching and learning movements within fresh expressions. Movements from:

- starting with creedal knowledge to starting with practical knowledge
- top-down courses taught by experts to bottom-up approaches that encourage participants to discover truth for themselves
- standardized courses to contextualized culturally relevant approaches – which very much fits with the underlying rationale for fresh expressions.

He suggests that instead of starting with basic doctrines, discipleship will tend to start with life questions. Responses to these questions will draw on Christian doctrine, thereby introducing the questioner to creedal knowledge. The focus on practical knowledge ensures that discipleship is for the whole of life. Commenting on Moynagh's thoughts on the website Share, Stuart Murray Williams helpfully points out that:

> Very often Jesus helped people realize that there were more important questions than the ones they were asking. People's questions may be the starting point, and we certainly need to listen very carefully rather than imposing our agenda or insisting on our starting points, but becoming a disciple often means learning to ask different questions.[30]

A third group of fresh expressions are choosing to develop disciples through a new monastic route. Mark Berry was keen to point out that 'we don't use programmes', saying at Safe Space in Telford that they practise daily rhythms and liturgies, Ignatian spiritual exercises and pilgrimage – which one could argue is actually a different form of programmed activity. Ian Mobsby explained how Moot has adopted a 'very spirituality focused approach to learning via "a creative and artistic discourse"'. The approach he says is:

> Very experiential – encouraging questing – encouraging questing of the imagination – inspiration from Walter Brueggemann's prophetic imagination and Berryman with Godly Play – encouraging changes in the imagination by encountering God – knowing God through experience of God – less about knowing facts about God – through wonderment exploration. Use of image and story are vital.[31]

---

30 www.sharetheguide.org/discipleship/principles/outline.

31 For more on new monasticism and fresh expressions, see G. Cray, I. Mobsby and A. Kennedy (eds), *New Monasticism as Fresh Expression of Church*, Norwich: Canterbury Press, 2010.

There is much good creative work being done to develop learning approaches that are culturally relevant and appropriate for disciple-making in a postmodern context. The approaches I encountered resonated strongly with the 'Discipling Model of Teaching' described by Sylvia Wilkey Collinson.[32] She says that this model has six key components. It is:

1 Relational.
2 Intentional (all members have a responsibility for learning).
3 Mainly informal and life related.
4 Typically communal.
5 Reciprocal (learning is mutual and collaborative).
6 Centrifugal in focus (disciples go out from community to be involved in service and mission and then return to reflect).

Alongside these components leaders have a responsibility for ensuring that learning has substance as well as style and honours the scriptures, creeds, theology and tradition of the wider Church. In intentionally missional churches, committed to making new disciples, the foundational beliefs of the Christian faith together with the key formative practices of Christian discipleship do need to be taught. The methods may well be similar to those advocated by Wilkey Collinson but the content needs to dig deep into the foundations of the scriptures and the Christian tradition.

## By their fruits you shall know them

As more fresh expressions form and grow, the healthy and fruitful examples are characterized by being God-centred, knowing their place well, being humble, developing indigenous leadership and having healthy disciple-forming communities.

So what factors lie behind unfruitful new ventures? Obviously where the characteristics that typify healthy fresh expressions are absent or neglected then newly forming church communities will

---

32 S. Wilkey Collinson: *Making Disciples*, Milton Keynes: Paternoster, 2004, p. 241.

struggle. So inattentiveness to God, especially in prayer and the reading of the scriptures, a rushed or partial attempt to know one's place, arrogance, a lack of indigenous leadership and discipleship as an add-on or afterthought will all stifle life and growth.

In addition, the following six factors may also contribute to unfruitful fresh expressions of Church.

1  **An unsuitable form.** This could result from an attempt to replicate someone else's good idea, forgetting that God is into creativity, not cloning. Alternatively the pioneer or planting team may have too fixed an idea of what Church should look like, and impose their views – repeating the mistakes of many a colonial missionary before.

2  **Partial expressions.** The debates around what are and are not fresh expressions will continue for some time to come. It is always helpful to remember that what are being sought are fresh expressions of *Church*. To be fully Church is to be one (united in Christian fellowship), holy (centred on God especially through worship), catholic (knowing one's place within the whole body of Christ) and apostolic (sent in mission). A risk with some emerging fresh expressions is that they are only partial expressions of Church – commendable new ventures in worship or particular missional activity, but not fully Church.

3  **A lack of planning and preparation.** With fresh expressions springing up all over the place there is a great temptation to rush into a new venture. Like seed sown in shallow soil, there may be an initial and quick spurt of life and growth, but without proper prayer, planning and preparation, the life and growth is likely to be short-lived. In Luke 14.28–29 we find a timely warning from Jesus:

> Suppose one of you wants to build a tower. Will he not first sit down and estimate the cost to see if he has enough money to complete it? For if he lays the foundation and is not able to finish it, everyone who sees it will ridicule him, saying, 'This fellow began to build and was not able to finish.' (NIV)

Having a flexible strategy for sustainability is important right from the beginning. So too is a counting of the costs involved – especially the personal costs alluded to earlier in this chapter and explored more fully in the following ones.

4 **Not remaining missional and a lack of ambition.** The UK landscape is littered with chapels and church buildings that were once centres of mission. The now empty or converted buildings bear sad testimony to churches that became insular and lost their missional heart and edge. This is a very real challenge for fresh expressions – to remain missional, a challenge that becomes more complex as new disciples are made who need nurturing.

One of the great strengths of many fresh expressions is that they have a great depth of community. This strength again brings the challenge to develop communities that are both deep and open. Without these twin characteristics there is a real risk of pioneering fresh expressions settling too soon. Some pioneers may wish to argue the positive virtue of smaller churches, and a case can be well made for this. But if the fresh expressions movement is serious about changing the landscape and seeing the kingdom come across Britain and beyond, in both the broken and the beautiful places, then there will need to be many, many such smaller churches.

If Steve Jobs wanted the Apple Corporation to make 'a dent in the universe',[33] why should those stepping out in response to the Great Commission not think big too?

5 **Lack of connections and support.** Just as a pioneer doing their own thing with no regard for the rest of the body of Christ is not good, so pioneers being left to struggle without proper oversight and support from the wider church is not right either. In a true mixed-economy church, fresh expressions will be welcomed as true partners in mission and given proper representation within the decision-making meetings and budgets of the denomination or stream of which they are part.

---

33 newmediaandmarketing.com/the-innovation-secrets-of-steve-jobs/marketing-innovation-2/.

6 **Spiritual opposition.** We began this chapter by reflecting on how the nature of fresh expressions needs to reflect the nature of God, and how fresh expressions are called to share in the work of God. The work of God will always attract opposition, both human and spiritual. There will be temptations as well as opposition – the ghost of the 1990s Sheffield-based *Nine O'clock Service* still haunts memories. For fresh expressions to remain healthy it is vital that they are wise to and discerning of both the forces that may seek to oppose them and the temptations that will come their way. The holiness as well as the hospitality of God is crucial.

This last risk factor takes us full circle and reminds us that if fresh expressions are to be true to their calling and bear fruit as they share in the *missio Dei*, then they need to be truly God-centred in everything they are and do.

## Further reading and resources

Atkins, M., *Resourcing Renewal*, Peterborough: Inspire, 2007.

Atkins, M., 'OPPS not OOPS!', *Methodist Recorder* 8014, 28 July 2011.

Bayes, P., Sledge T., Holbrook, J., Rylands, M. and Seeley, M., *Mission-Shaped Parish: Traditional Church in a Changing World*, London: Church House Publishing, 2006.

Cray, G., Mobsby, I. and Kennedy, A. (eds), *New Monasticism as Fresh Expression of Church*, Norwich: Canterbury Press, 2010.

Croft, S. and Mobsby, I. (eds), *Fresh Expressions in the Sacramental Tradition*, London: Canterbury Press, 2009.

Davison, A. and Milbank, A., *For the Parish: A Critique of Fresh Expressions*, London: SCM Press, 2010.

Gray-Reeves, M. and Perham, M., *The Hospitality of God*, London: SPCK, 2011.

Greene, M. and Cotterell, T., *Imagine: Let My People Grow*, Milton Keynes: Authentic Media, 2006.

Inge, J., *A Christian Theology of Place*, Aldershot: Ashgate, 2003.

Langrish, M., 'Dynamics of Community', in J. Martineau et al., *Changing Rural Life*, Norwich: Canterbury Press, 2004.

Lawrence, L., *The Word in Place*, London: SPCK, 2009.

Methodist Church, *Share this Feast*, 2006.

Shier-Jones, A., *Pioneer Ministry and Fresh Expressions of Church*, London: SPCK, 2009.

Smith, A., *God-Shaped Mission*, Norwich: Canterbury Press, 2008.

Stott, J., *The Message of Acts*, Leicester: InterVarsity Press, 1990.

Wilkey Collinson, S., *Making Disciples*, Milton Keynes, Paternoster, 2004.

## DVDs

Fresh Expressions: *Expressions: The DVD*
Fresh Expressions: *Expressions: Making a Difference*

## Websites

www.freshexpressions.org.uk
www.sharetheguide.org

# 5

# God's Call to Pioneer

## Introduction

The impact of increasingly rapid global change is being felt everywhere. Whether you are reading this book in the throbbing departure lounge at Heathrow airport, a teashop beside a loch in the Scottish highlands or a vicarage study in a Welsh market town, change is all around you. Every institution in our society recognizes this – including the Church – and most are trying hard to work out how to adapt in order to flourish. It is at times like ours that those who are comfortable with change emerge as valuable assets to communities and organizations. Not all change is good, but Christians who embrace change as a God-given, defining feature of life are able to see within it the potential for new opportunities. In the Christian community we might call such people prophets: those who are able to articulate the vision of God's alternative (redemptive) future. If these people are able to move beyond simply articulating a vision of an alternative future and to work with others to enable such a future to emerge, we might also call them pioneers. Pioneers – those who can speak authentically of God's future for the Church and the wider world *and* draw others into moving towards this future – are emerging throughout the Church in the UK. The language of pioneer may not be used across the denominations, but the nature of the vision and the shape of the activities in which these women and men are engaged share certain characteristics.

Pioneers are a gift of God to his Church. This is particularly clear at times of change and perceived uncertainty. As with much of the work of God, the Church often takes a little while to catch up and to put its shoulder to the right part of the wheel. Thankfully many parts of the Church are alive to the potential of pioneers in their midst and are actively seeking to identify, train, enable, deploy, support and encourage them. Since the publication of the groundbreaking *Mission-Shaped Church* (MSC) report in 2004, the Church of England has endorsed lay and ordained pioneer ministry, with the result that theological colleges throughout the UK are offering routes through training for those who have been identified as pioneers. In a similar way, the Methodist Church is facilitating the training and deployment of pioneers through Venture FX.[1] The Church Mission Society[2] is also offering training for lay pioneers, and nationally the Mission-Shaped Ministry[3] course and ReSource[4] have proved hugely effective in equipping an increasing number of people – lay and ordained – for undertaking pioneering work in their local communities. Other denominations are offering similar approaches to training and support. The national picture is encouraging. There is a long way to go but we appear to be heading in the right direction.

The widespread recognition that the Church needs pioneers at this time, and the efforts involved in identifying, training, deploying, and supporting them, raises many questions. In the following three chapters I address some of these. This chapter will consider the identity of the pioneer, encourage readers to ask themselves whether they might be called to pioneer, and examine some of the qualities we would expect to see in those undertaking pioneering ministry. Since pioneers work alongside others to form community or initiate new ventures, Chapter 6 will address questions relating to the nature and shape of Christian community and the 'how to' of getting something new off the ground. Chapter 7 will look at sustainability and consider how pioneers and the fresh expressions of Church they facilitate and serve can be equipped for the long haul.

---

1 See www.venturefxpioneer.blogspot.com.
2 See www.pioneer.cms-uk.org.
3 See www.missionshapedministry.org.
4 See www.resourcemission.com.

In order to address these issues, I worked closely with a research group of Christians who are currently involved in practice and reflection on pioneering (more on this group at the end of Chapter 7). I asked my research group to complete a questionnaire focused on fresh expressions and pioneer ministry. I had a 100 per cent response rate and found the range of insights very helpful, in both consolidating and challenging my own thinking on pioneering in the UK.

The question of how to present the results of the questionnaires provoked a good deal of thought. I could have looked for common threads and written a summary highlighting the main points: or perhaps pulled out a series of particularly punchy quotes and woven them into the text to illustrate or support my own conclusions. But since I am a serial blogger and a signed-up member of the Facebook generation, I opted for a comment-thread approach. As I read and reread the responses, I couldn't imagine a more effective way of communicating their insight and power than including them in the text as they stood, to speak for themselves. I hope the inclusion of selections of the research group's undiluted responses will broaden the reach and deepen the rootedness of these three chapters. Because of pressure on space I haven't included every response to every question. I invite you to engage with them as a reflective exercise, allowing each to shape the others and simultaneously your own understanding of and feelings towards pioneering.

I believe that each Christian has particular, God-given gifts and a unique calling. I think it is possible for all of us to be involved in pioneering, and my approach to teaching mission and pioneer ministry rests on the assumption that everyone has the capacity to engage in forms of kingdom innovation in their local situations. This is not the same as saying that all are pioneers. While holding that all have the ability to exercise creativity in worship and witness, it seems clear to me that God equips and calls particular people to focus on pioneering. Pioneers, however, are not always those we might imagine.

## Am I a pioneer?

Pioneers in the Church are often blighted by an unhelpful stereo-type that goes something like this: pioneers are predominantly young, white, male, middle-class, well-educated, sporty, char-ismatic (both in personality and spirituality), theologically con-servative, ordained and intent on planting large, lively churches peopled by those who are rather like themselves. Like all stereo-types, this one is, of course, highly questionable. Pioneers are teens and grandparents and everything in between. They come from a range of ethnic backgrounds and are male and female. They are found in every social class and may hold a PhD or have no formal qualifications at all. Some eat, sleep and breathe football, surfing or cycling. Others are more at home with a book and a bar of chocolate, or at the theatre with a glass of wine. While some lead from the front and are bubbling over with charisma, others lead from elsewhere – preferring quiet pastoral conversations to up-front presentations. Pioneers are found in house churches, cathe-drals, parish churches, mega-churches and retreat centres. They are Baptists, Methodists, Catholics, Anglicans, United Reformed, Assemblies of God, Vineyard, New Frontiers and any number of other free churches. Some might be ordained and hold a ministe-rial title such as pastor, deacon, presbyter or bishop. Many more are not ordained and never will be. Some will be called to plant large churches, others will be catalysts for small communities or networks, and yet others for temporary projects or for initiatives that bring people together around a particular cause or issue. Pioneers are everywhere. They don't fit into neat boxes, and the selection of those in my research group was designed to reflect this. What pioneers have in common is the desire and ability to work with others to make something happen that wasn't happen-ing before. They think differently but crucially they *do* something different. What emerges might be entirely 'new' or, perhaps more likely, a new way of doing something old. One thing is for sure: pioneers *act*. And they act out of a belief that things could be better than they are right now.

If you haven't asked yourself the question at the head of this section already, I would encourage you to ask it now. Since we have already established that pioneers do not fit any kind of stereotype, it's possible that you are one. Below I have set out some of the responses I received from my research group on the question of who the pioneer might be. As you read through them and are prompted to consider how pioneers think and act, I urge you to reflect on whether God might be equipping and calling you to be a pioneer in the Church at this time. If you are already involved in pioneering work, either as a pioneer or as a facilitator, I hope the responses will not only resonate with your experience but also provide a useful challenge – perhaps highlighting areas where further thought or effort would be fruitful.

## Comment feed

### Responses to the question: 'Who is a pioneer?'

## Beth Keith

A pioneer is someone who sees future possibilities and works to bring them to reality. She is not fazed by the problems or issues, but can imagine something new, something different, something alive. The Church needs people who, with the Spirit's inspiration, can imagine and build Church in new ways and in new contexts.

## Janet Sutton

The key characteristic is being spiritually equipped to discern God's will, then having the courage, faithfulness and fortitude to follow it through. Pioneers also need patience – which ironically isn't a characteristic I have identified in most of the pioneers I know! Pioneering is slow work, which other people are often inclined to misunderstand. Patience is required because it takes time for Church to emerge. But pioneers also have to be patient with those who find new ideas threatening, intimidating or downright scary.

## Chris Howson

To some extent all Christians are pioneers. Each day and in each new situation and context, Christians are asked to work out afresh what it means to show God's love. For the Church to demonstrate that it is part of God's reign, it needs to display a wide range of personalities and characteristics. It needs those who have courage, those who can see how a situation can be turned around and are prepared to act, even at great personal cost. It needs people with great patience. By this I mean that communities of love are built over time, respectful of the differing faith journeys of their members. We cannot enter a place and expect everything to change overnight. We have to notice what God is already doing in a place, we have to respect the work of others with different insights from our own, and we have to spend time really getting to know a place. This requires patience. We also need people who demonstrate God's love in their day-to-day living. We must be the change we want to see in the world. This means opening our lives to those in need, and living countercultural lives.

## Ellen Louden

Pioneers are alternative thinkers who are prepared to live on the fringes of society and culture – who cannot bear to live in the cultural centre – who shout from the edge and challenge systems – including the Church. For me this is what the Church should be doing all the time but I understand that some of us struggle with that.

## Bishop John Went

The letter to the Hebrews describes Jesus as a pioneer, a word used of a military task force clearing a way through difficult terrain or hostile territory, making a way for others to follow in their footsteps. All Christians are called to follow in the footsteps of Jesus, our pioneer, but the Church at this time especially needs leaders who can inspire and encourage others in making that pioneering journey of faith. Pioneering is essentially an apostolic ministry. Those who undertake it must be prepared to break new ground for the gospel and to reach out to the increasing numbers in our society who are totally unchurched. It is about building bridges. It is also about risk-taking. Pioneers must be prepared for some initiatives to fail in the hope of finding ways that do connect with people who have no knowledge of Jesus Christ. I see Saint Paul as a pioneer par excellence. He was extremely focused, both on the people he was trying to reach and on the message he was seeking to communicate. He was strategic in his approach. He was a great evangelist and missionary and yet he believed totally in releasing the gifts of the whole people of God. So a pioneer in today's Church needs to be a gifted leader, yet not a one-person band – rather, someone who is able to harness the gifts of others in the missionary enterprise.

## Ben Norton

For me a pioneer is someone who lives in a state of constant restlessness in their spirit, knowing that 'business as usual' will never get the job done. They are a person for whom the love of God must be communicated at all costs with a total disregard for the risks involved. The pioneer will have to fight certain battles – the key thing is knowing which ones. The Church needs risk-takers, people who are willing to give up houses, jobs, money and all other false securities in order to rediscover the Church in places it has either ceased to exist or has yet to be born.

## David Wilkinson

A pioneer is someone who is called by God who has a vocation to pioneering ministry. I believe this is a gift given by God. It is built upon certain personality and characteristic types, which are about a degree of self-confidence, trust in the unusual workings of the Holy Spirit, courage to take risks and the ability to communicate vision to others.

## Ben Edson

Being a pioneer is a mindset and a way of being.

## Ian Meredith

A pioneer explores new territories, takes other with them, is a risk-taker, is willing to try new things and is an experimenter. The Church needs pioneers but it needs them to be team players.

## Jo Cox

Pioneers are creative catalysts (or deliberately divisive influences – discuss).

## Joe Knight

I think it's important to establish first that Jesus is the pioneer. Everyone else follows. Jesus leads the way into new, uncharted lands, and I like to think of pioneers as those who follow Christ on the margins between the frontier between lands known and lands unknown, creating maps along the way. Therefore ultimately the Church is in need of people who are like Jesus, people who have 'dropped their nets' to follow him and have become his disciples, his Talmidim. These three factors are important for pioneers: i) to have prophetic vision – to see what God is doing in the 'not yet' of our today; ii) to be humble and teachable – being shaped in the place of prayer; and iii) to be courageous servants: willing to be the change they long to see take place.

## John Drane

I want to say that anyone can be a pioneer, once they are given permission to engage creatively with the missional challenge. Since creativity is the first attribute of God in scripture, and people are made in God's image, there is no such thing as an uncreative person – though many think they are uncreative, more likely their creativity has been denied by being forced into other people's boxes. The notion of mixed economy certainly doesn't allow us to say pioneers have a certain personality type, as that would be to downgrade some ways of being in favour of others. I'm tempted to say something really old-fashioned, like 'a passion for the lost' is the main characteristic of the pioneer.

## Mark Berry

The pioneer shines a critical and creative light on all aspects of the Church and community, including its leadership structure and practice . . . Whatever they are doing, pioneers will do it in a way that is creative, challenges the status quo and breaks down barriers. Pioneers will always be asking the question: 'But what if . . .?' They will always get excited about new possibilities, opportunities and ideas.

## Sue Wallace

A pioneer is someone who can imagine possibilities that do not exist, someone who does not see the boundaries that most of us see and who can imagine taking almost anything they come across and using it to further the kingdom of God. Pioneers are more likely to hang around in dark corners or on the edges, or to patrol the margins looking for those who are willing to listen to the gospel. Pioneers are not afraid to go beyond those margins bringing the light of Christ with them. Those pioneers who are not ordained will have friar-like qualities, being willing to share the gospel without shame, fear or compromise and yet also be people of prayer who gather communities of prayer around them.

## Ian Bell

Pioneers are willing to take gospel risks that may be seriously disturbing to some, are unlikely to lead to a place of safety or comfort, but are consistent with the radical kingdom movement of Jesus and are connected with the inherited tradition of the wider and historic Church. Pioneers are able to engage with a culture or community that may be similar to or different from their own, and articulate what the good news might mean there. They are able to pay close attention to the context in which they are called to work, and to share the good news in a way that relates best to that context.

The qualities we find in the research group's responses do not make for an exhaustive list. And it is important to say that not all pioneers will possess all these qualities or act in all the ways highlighted. We must also take care to point out that there are plenty of people who are characterized by combinations of the above and who never do anything vaguely pioneering. However, the list concurs with much of my own experience and is helpful in placing on the table a significant number of the characteristics we might expect to see in the lives and work of pioneers. In this sense it offers a starting point for reflecting on the possibility of the reader's own call to pioneer. For those already engaged in pioneering, this list may act as a helpful resource to accompany reflection on their current understanding of the nature and shape of their pioneering ministry and how this might evolve in the months and years ahead.

When discussing *who* the pioneer is, some commentators have used the word entrepreneur. Let's look at this association.

## Mission entrepreneurs?

The guidelines for the selection of ordained pioneer ministers within the Church of England state: 'Bishops' Advisers should watch for candidates who have the necessary vision and gifts to be missionary entrepreneurs.'[5] This book is written with a wider readership in mind than those within the Church of England. However, what is fascinating here is the deliberate use of the word entrepreneur as an aid to imagining and communicating the type of ministry this part of the Church sees as necessary. The word itself draws a mixed response when used in conjunction with Christian ministry. Although some are happy with it, more often than not it prompts responses ranging from discomfort to fervent objection. No doubt this is due to its association with a worldly approach to wealth creation for personal gain – fostered by TV programmes like *The Apprentice* and *Dragons' Den*. While the instinctive reaction of many Christians might be to steer clear of the word and its apparently un-Christian connotations, it is nevertheless true that many of the characteristics associated with entrepreneurship are the characteristics we see displayed in pioneers.

At this point it seems worthwhile highlighting the fact that the Western Church appears to have less of a problem importing bureaucratic or managerial terminology into its vocabulary. Obvious examples in my own denomination, the Church of England, are Ministry *Division*, Church *Commissioners* and Diocesan *Boards* of Finance. My point here is that if, as a Church, we are content to embrace labels and concepts drawn from bureaucratic and management terminology, we might be prompted to question what lies at the heart of our reservations about using the language of entrepreneurship. My own research at Durham University

---

5 *Guidelines for the Identification, Training and Deployment of Ordained Pioneer Ministers*, Archbishops' Council, Ministry Division, 2005.

has involved an attempt to construct an understanding of the word that is theologically acceptable and useful when applied to Christian ministry.

The starting point was the work of Bill Bolton and John Thompson, who define the entrepreneur as: 'A person who habitually creates and innovates to build something of recognized value around perceived opportunities.'[6] In his Grove booklet Bolton suggests that, 'Releasing the entrepreneurial talent among God's people is the greatest task facing the church today.'[7] Although I have some reservations about whether this is the *greatest* task, I share Bolton's sense of urgency about the Church's need to find and release those whom God has gifted and called to be pioneers. Given the mission task that the Church in the UK currently faces, there is a pressing need to identify and release the pioneers in our midst – and the pioneers are, in fact, those members of the body of Christ who possess entrepreneurial gifts. Pioneers use their entrepreneurial ability to work with others to build up the Church, to seek out and serve the lost and to further the building of the kingdom.

Although I find Bolton's definition hugely helpful, in the context of Christian ministry in general and pioneering in particular, I feel it lacks a crucial communal element. Christian pioneering is essentially and fundamentally communal. The people of God do not need a few talented pioneering heroes. What is required are thousands of pioneers who lead by example and act to galvanize local churches into entrepreneurial communities capable of habitually creating and innovating to build things of recognized value around perceived local opportunities. Apostolic ministry and early Christian leadership in the book of Acts have been discussed in Chapters 1 and 3. There is a clear overlap between such ministries and the notion of the entrepreneur.

During my research into entrepreneurship I conducted a survey of the relevant literature. A number of characteristics and behav-

---

6 B. Bolton and J. Thompson, *Entrepreneurs: Talent, Temperament, Technique*, 2nd edn, Elsevier Butterworth-Heinemann, 2004, p. 16.

7 B. Bolton, *The Entrepreneur and the Church*, Cambridge: Grove Books, 2006, p. 4.

iours common to entrepreneurs emerged. Although not every entrepreneur will exhibit all of them, we are likely to observe combinations. Since pioneers demonstrate entrepreneurial qualities, the following paragraph is included to help the reader think through his or her own capacity for operating as a mission entrepreneur/pioneer. According to the literature, entrepreneurs:

Think; Put together new combinations of already existing materials; Produce something novel and innovative; Habitually create; Systematically innovate; Make (difficult) decisions; Are comfortable with change; Identify opportunities; Exercise (good) judgement; Take risks; Focus (resulting in something of recognized value being built/achieved); See differently (have a different view); Have the strength to challenge the view of others; Change knowledge; Create social networks; Are trustworthy and persuasive in their networks; Are fluent in a range of skills; Have and exercise wisdom; Are able to gain information; Are bold; Are ingenious; Are leaders; Are persistent; Build something of recognized value.

There is a lively debate about whether entrepreneurs are born or made. This is important because if they are 'born', our key question will be. 'How do you spot them?' And if they are 'made', then our efforts will be focused on attempting to train and shape as many as possible. Advocates for both points of view are articulate and vocal. In my opinion, therefore, it makes sense to devote attention to both 'spotting' and 'training'. Our churches and communities must be encouraged to work towards becoming places in which entrepreneurial flair – the ability to spot opportunities, articulate vision, draw together resources, work with others to achieve something of recognized worth (taking the inevitable risks en route) – is valued and encouraged. Putting it simply: we will spot more entrepreneurs if we make it easy for them to do their thing. As well as becoming environments in which entrepreneurial flair is highly regarded, churches could gain much by offering training aimed at developing and honing some of the skills, strengths and competencies set out in the paragraph above.

As you reflect on your own reaction to the possibility of the word entrepreneur being an asset in our understanding of the Christian life and the call to be pioneering in the current context, I again offer the responses of the research group to this question.

## Comment feed

> Responses to the question: 'How is the word entrepreneur used in relation to Christian pioneering?'

### Ben Norton

The terms entrepreneur and pioneer are very closely knit. In my opinion they are one and the same. An entrepreneur is someone who will be able to think about things from a different angle, to produce a new perspective.

### Bishop John Went

In as much as entrepreneurial skills are about taking initiatives, risk-taking, being creative, reaching out in new ways, these are valuable skills for pioneer ministry. However, sometimes entrepreneurs have a tendency to be sole-operators, not good at listening to others, so I would wish to qualify entrepreneur with the ability to listen and to collaboratively involve others in the mission task.

### Chris Howson

I loathe the use of the word entrepreneur. We do not need to borrow more terms from the market – our faith has been privatized enough as it is! The word entrepreneur has too many connotations with taking risks for personal gain. The risks that a Christian takes are at personal cost, not gain. If one looks at contemporary understanding of the entrepreneur it is associated with programmes such as *The Apprentice* and *Dragons' Den*. These programmes reflect the ruthlessness of modern capitalist society, and are inherently confrontational and combative. Pioneer ministry must be sensitive and constructive. Collaboration and solidarity are terms that might be more helpful, and may help reduce some of the more negative and individualistic assumptions that must be overcome when already using terms like pioneer.

## David Wilkinson

I like the word entrepreneur. In a business context it speaks of someone who builds for the future, who sees new possibilities, who is prepared to take risks. I can see how some within the Church would react against it but there is creativity with entrepreneurship which I think we get at in pioneer ministry.

## Ian Meredith

I run a business as well as being active in ministry (although I don't agree with the distinction). I am entrepreneurial in both. The entrepreneurial spirit can be effective in pioneer contexts and also helpful for sustainable models of pioneer leadership where funding may not be available.

## Janet Sutton

Entrepreneur is not a word I would use in relation to my own pioneering ministry. I would prefer to use a word like prophetic – a term which partly explains why pioneers are often treated by traditional elements of the Church with suspicion. Prophets can see how change can be achieved. Those who are reluctant to change do not welcome this. I suppose my own role is entrepreneurial as I began more or less with a blank piece of paper and a timespan in which to achieve something. But it is not a definition that sits comfortably with me.

## Jo Cox

The current pioneers are entrepreneurs. People with a passion and vision and drive to begin something new for a local context or part of society. Entrepreneur brings with it the notion of creativity, invention, learning from failure and pushing boundaries.

## Joe Knight

Entrepreneurs make things happen. They have the ability to dream and also to organize. They are willing to take risks. They also have the ability to enthuse and empower others to join in. Not all entrepreneurs are pioneers though, and vice versa. In ministry, the word entrepreneur helps explain the depth and commitment of the word pioneer. Pioneering is about establishing something that is sustainable, meets ongoing needs and generates circles of community. Pioneer ministry, inclusive of a sense of entrepreneurship, helps keep the pioneer grounded; creatively finding new ways to make the small steps that ultimately see dreams fulfilled.

## John Drane

I have no problem with the use of the word entrepreneur in relation to ministry, just so long as we don't imagine it excludes some people.

## Jonny Baker

An entrepreneur is someone who builds something. And I like people that spot opportunities or gaps and are able to create something there. It's an exciting word. For those of us who remember

Margaret Thatcher it is also tainted with capitalist overtones, but it's pretty clear that it's not being used in that way in the context of mission.

## Robert Warren

Entrepreneurs are not often team players and can be driven rather than called. Servants and vocation are more important aspects of ministry that need exploring.

## Ian Bell

I understand the reason why the word is used, but I struggle to feel entirely comfortable with it. Pioneers must be people who are able to see opportunities and develop them where others might not. They need to have the inner resources as well as the motivation and ability to make things happen, to take initiatives and to work with others to create something from nothing. But it is difficult to detach the word from the world of business and commerce – which has sufficient connotations of consumerism and materialism to make it somewhat unhelpful. Maybe 'spiritual entrepreneur' is slightly better?

## Sue Wallace

Entrepreneurs take risks and pioneers also need to take risks while trying to put flesh on the bones of new ideas. We also need to be aware that entrepreneurs often fail, so we need to be understanding with those pioneers who are bruised by their own failure.

## We need each other

Earlier in the chapter I set out a bogus stereotype that blights pioneers in some contexts. Another unhelpful stereotype is that pioneers are only interested in the new and the fresh and have scant regard for anything traditional or institutional. My experience of pioneers across the UK leads me to believe that this is simply not the case. Among those called to pioneer, there is a deep attentiveness to the riches of our shared Christian heritage and a willingness to understand and honour traditional approaches to worship and ministry. As we consider and weigh the need for new forms of Church alongside the fullness of what has been handed to us by previous generations, we must shout loudly about the fundamental importance of excellent communication and genuine humility.

I spent three years on the staff at Gloucester Cathedral while being simultaneously involved in pioneering work in the city centre. The Cathedral's Chapter and congregation were incredibly supportive of the pioneering work, and through a lively and respectful dialogue both the emerging community and the cathedral learnt a huge amount from one another. Dialogue, patience, love, mutual respect and common prayer are key factors in ensuring that inherited and emerging forms of Church mutually benefit from one another. In *Church After Christendom*, Stuart Murray writes, 'The brightest hope for church after Christendom is a symbiotic relationship between inherited and emerging churches. We need each other.'[8] On the same note, in *The Future of the Parish System*, Steven Croft – the current bishop of Sheffield – writes:

> The most traditional of congregations needs to be connected with the cutting edge. This ministry of connection is vital if fresh expressions are to remain part of the Church of England and not spin off into their own denomination . . . It is also vital

---

8 S. Murray, *Church After Christendom*, Milton Keynes: Paternoster Press, 2004, p. 122.

for the traditional Church to have the life and vitality of the new mission movements.[9]

The most effective pioneers understand this. They also understand that more often than not it will be up to them to demonstrate a mature willingness to listen before their voice and vision can be heard. If you are the pioneer, I would encourage you to pray for and nurture the gifts of patience and wisdom and to practise the virtue of courage. You will need to discern when to keep silent and when to speak up boldly. You will need to remember that you have much to learn – while also recognizing that it might be the articulation of your fresh perspective on things that prompts the people of God to rethink inherited practices for the benefit of the lost and the broken. Most Christians in the UK are able to admit that *any* form of worship and church activity – in the mainline denominations as well as the independent churches – has the potential to operate as a frustrating barrier to fresh thinking, especially if that thinking challenges the status quo or general levels of comfort and security. At various points in each of our lives we will receive the call to leave our places of comfort and security and journey to new and unfamiliar lands. This can be difficult to hear and even harder to act out. Pioneers are part of that call to the wider Church, but they must remain open to hearing that call in their own lives. I asked my research group to say something about the need for pioneers to strike a balance between honouring what has been received and articulating what might need to emerge. Their responses may help you to reflect on your own view of this important question and perhaps challenge you to think a little differently.

9 S. Croft (ed.), *The Future of the Parish System: Shaping the Church of England in the 21st Century*, London: Church House Publishing, 2006, p. 77.

## Comment feed

Responses to the question: 'What balance might the pioneer need to strike between honouring what has been received and being a catalyst for new understandings of Church and faith?'

### Ellen Louden

As we move forward naturally we should do it in a kind and generous way – bringing people alongside us. I think we need to help people to name and own their present situations and identify if there are bits of this that need to change to move more purposely forward. This purpose needs to be steeped in gospel values and not those of an ever-changing world. I am not sure striving for the new is of any worth if people don't have a language for their present.

### Mark Berry

Pioneers should not be people who simply discard the things of tradition; they value those things as rich resources. However, they look at the past with creative eyes – as a source of inspiration and not as a static thing. Pioneers are treasure hunters but not collectors. They seek wisdom, beauty and meaning in the past in order to enrich the present and the future. They don't put the past on a pedestal never to be touched or changed.

### Ben Edson

If the pioneer is wise, he or she can be the catalyst for the renewal of the tradition. They need to move beyond the perceived binary opposites of 'fresh expressions of Church' and 'traditional Church' and recognize that these two work together. The one resources the other and vice versa.

## Ben Norton

The pioneer is bilingual and must be able to speak with authority and integrity in the inherited Church as well as speaking fluently in the language of those who have never been to church. As a pioneer I am rooted in the Church of England because of the rich heritage that has been passed down the generations. This heritage now allows me to step out in the name of the Church, and in my experience people have responded positively to new and fresh ways of doing things.

## Beth Keith

In discussions I have found that many pioneers find the balancing act between honouring received traditions and catalyzing new practices extremely difficult to negotiate. In some cases this is the hardest part of their role. While pioneers expect to spend time negotiating with and educating the existing church community about mission, they were not prepared for this to become their principal challenge.

## Bishop John Went

If a pioneer is working within – but on the edge – of an inherited mode of Church in order to pioneer new ways of being Church, it is very important to be able to affirm traditional church members and to be able to acknowledge that God meets with people through inherited church structures and patterns of worship. In that way the pioneer will be likely to have the prayer backing of the inherited Church and there will be a sense (important) of congregations owning the new work. The pioneer needs to be able to help more traditional church members to see the need to explore fresh ways of being Church and witnessing to the gospel. In this sense pioneering is a considerably more demanding ministry than more traditional church ministry. It involves an ability to inhabit both traditional church space and more innovative ways of being Church.

## Chris Howson

Pioneers must never forget that they are connected to the whole family of God. If they are not working collaboratively – or even working in isolation from the local church communities – then they may well be wasting a lot of energy, and storing up problems for later on. The more a pioneer can work with what already exists, the more likely it is that the project will be more sustainable, and be able to create a base that may re-energize the wider body of Christ.

## David Wilkinson

It seems to me that we always overstress the honouring of what has been received because we're afraid of what is new. It is right that we honour what we've received through scripture and in tradition, but we also need to understand that God is active in his world and the Holy Spirit is continually doing new things.

## Janet Sutton

The Church is the body of Christ, not a human institution. However, much of what we learn within our denominations is opinion and interpretation. Part of the pioneer's role is to fathom where institutionalism ends and truth begins – and to practise what he or she preaches. This does not always make pioneers popular. What I would defend is the need for serious theology to be done alongside exploratory practice. All that we do as pioneers should be justified theologically.

## Joe Knight

If we have a *new* understanding of Church that doesn't honour and connect us with other parts of the body of Christ, then our understanding of Church is seriously flawed. I find Jesus' prayer in John 17 inspiring to help with this balancing act. It is God's intention that his people – the Church – are to be 'one' in the same way as the Trinity. And we see that the Trinity is full of creative diversity and beauty, with a mysterious interdependence between the Father, Son and Spirit. The Trinity is relational and embodies love itself. And this is the identity to which the Church is called, so that 'the world may know' the fullness and reality of God. Mission is made void when the Church isn't expressing the likeness of the Trinity. This means that we need to be aware of our motives as we explore new understandings of Church and faith. It also means that we should not let inherited expressions of Church hold us back from seeking the new. It is tempting to water down new understandings or expressions of Church for fear of not honouring what's been received. But this ends up honouring no one. Honouring is a case of loving those who don't understand, and running with all your might with those who do.

## John Drane

It depends how we define 'what has been received'. If it's things like how many times you're supposed to genuflect or what sort of music you should have, then we need to recognize that it's all culturally conditioned – which doesn't mean these traditions are irrelevant today, but that there are other ways of expressing the same underlying realities in terms of worship and so on. I think we need to get back to a minimalist account of what is received (Jesus!) while recognizing that in 2,000 years of history our forebears must have discovered something useful, so we need to learn from them. But learning from them rather than always copying them in the details.

## Jonny Baker

The metaphor I like to use around this is 'faithful improvisation'. The best improvisations come from those who are immersed in the tradition, whether in music or drama or theology. It is essential that pioneers know where they are coming from and have a deep repertoire of missiology, theology, ministry, liturgy and so on, which will enable their imaginings and improvisations to have depth and to be authentic. That is not to say that the traditions don't need ruptures – pioneers like Saint Francis have certainly brought these before. If we are going to talk about balance though, the real issue in terms of balance is that there isn't a good balance in the Church towards risk, creativity and imagination – it's conservative, cautious and risk-averse! The whole environment needs shifting.

## Robert Warren

It is vital that pioneers see themselves as bearers of the Christian heritage, not least as many drawn to a fresh expressions approach may tend to throw the baby out with the bath water. Those called to lead a fresh expression need to be deeply rooted in the Christian heritage otherwise, like much of the New (House) Church, what is created may be relevant to the present culture at the expense of selling out to it.

## Sue Wallace

Pioneers should devote time both to understanding the culture, and to understanding the treasures found within the traditions of the historical Church. Not in order to use them off-the-shelf in a pre-packaged manner, but because having a toolbox of useful tactics from a variety of Christian traditions enables pioneers to be more creative in their thinking.

## Stephen Lindridge

A pioneer for me doesn't have a theological, sociological or spiritual demographical stereotype. Those who see a need, hear God's whisper, just feel something must be done . . . and then go about the kingdom's business of making disciples of Jesus Christ and nurturing that new community of faith in a virgin context. That's a pioneer!

## Conclusion

Pioneers are one of the gifts that God gives to his Church. This is particularly apparent at times of change or uncertainty. Pioneers plant new forms of Church for a changing culture, but their work is not limited to this. They are also found initiating projects, rethinking outreach and creating resources. Pioneers do not fit into neat boxes, they defy stereotypes and are found throughout the Church. They are entrepreneurs in the sense that they are able to think differently, spot opportunities, make unusual connections, focus on the task and work with others to build something of recognized value for the kingdom. Previous experience of pioneering might sometimes be helpful but it is not a prerequisite – God often calls surprising people to undertake kingdom work. Pioneers are aware of the value of our shared Christian heritage and they broker newness through a process of faithful improvisation. Pioneers are good listeners and are committed to ongoing, humble, prayerful dialogue with the wider Church.

Prayer is a good note on which to conclude this chapter. S. D. Gordon wrote, 'The greatest thing anyone can do for God or people is pray.' Prayer is the key to being a disciple of Jesus, and pioneers know that in order to be 'sent out' they must be shaped in the place of prayer. Pioneers are men and women who commit themselves day by day to a careful discipline of prayer and attention to scripture. In the doing of this, they allow themselves to be shaped by the Spirit of God in order that their characters, thoughts, words and actions might be increasingly conformed to those of Christ. This attention to prayer will result in the following words of Jesus becoming a reality in the hearts, minds and lives of the pioneer: 'I am the vine; you are the branches. If you remain in me and I in you, you will bear much fruit; apart from me you can do nothing' (John 15.5 NIV).


## Further reading

Archbishops' Council, *Mission-Shaped Church*, London: Church House Publishing, 2004.

Bolton, B. and Thompson, J., *Entrepreneurs: Talent, Temperament, Technique*, 2nd edn, Elsevier Butterworth-Heinemann, 2004.

Bolton, B., *The Entrepreneur and the Church*, Cambridge: Grove Books, 2006.

Croft, S. (et al), *Evangelism in a Spiritual Age: Communicating Faith in a Changing Culture*, London: Church House Publishing, 2005.

Croft, S. (ed.), *The Future of the Parish System: Shaping the Church of England in the 21st Century*, London: Church House Publishing, 2006.

Croft, S. (ed.), *Mission-Shaped Questions*, London: Church House Publishing, 2008.

Drucker, P. F., *Innovation and Entrepreneurship*, Oxford: Elsevier, 1985.

Gibbs, E. and Bolger, R., *Emerging Churches*, London: SPCK, 2006.

Lawrence, J., *Growing Leaders: Reflections on Leadership, Life and Jesus*, Oxford: Bible Reading Fellowship, 2004.

Male, D. (ed.), *Pioneers for Life: Explorations in Theology and Wisdom for Pioneering Leaders*, Oxford: Bible Reading Fellowship, 2011.

Murray, S., *Church After Christendom*, Milton Keynes: Paternoster Press, 2004.

Myers, J. R., *Organic Community: Creating a Place Where People Naturally Connect*, Grand Rapids: Baker Books, 2007.

Rowland, D. and Higgs, M., *Sustaining Change: Leadership that Works*, San Francisco: Jossey-Bass, 2008.

Shier-Jones, A., *Pioneer Ministry and Fresh Expressions of Church*, London: SPCK, 2009.

Simms, M. K., *Faith Entrepreneurs: Empowering People by Faith, Nonprofit Organizational Leadership, and Entrepreneurship*, Lincoln, NE: iUniverse, 2006.

Volland, M., *Through the Pilgrim Door: Pioneering a Fresh Expression of Church*, Eastbourne: Survivor, 2009.

Ward, F., *Lifelong Learning: Theological Education and Supervision*, London: SCM Press, 2005.

# 6

# How to Pioneer a Fresh Expression of Church

## Introduction

Pioneering anything at all, from a new worship service or evangelism resource, to a community project, a small-group initiative or a fresh expression of Church, requires a number of ingredients. The focus of this chapter is on pioneering a fresh expression in a cross-cultural context (although many of the principles will be relevant to any act of pioneering), and it is intended to help you think through and plan for the fresh expression that God might be calling you to establish. What follows is a consideration of the groundwork out of which a vision for a healthy and sustainable fresh expression might begin to emerge. This is not a how-to guide in the sense that if you follow the instructions correctly it will lead to the construction of a sustainable fresh expression. Rather what is offered here are principles for generating a well-informed vision for a fresh expression. Like any principles, those set out below will need to be properly interpreted and applied in the context in which you find yourself. They are based on experience as well as common sense, and have emerged out of dialogue with pioneer church planters around the UK, shaped by prayer and through engagement with scripture, and informed by interaction with relevant literature.

Developing a vision, gaining wider support and understanding what resources are available are the essence of the groundwork for planting a fresh expression. These areas are intimately related and will emerge out of a process of prayerful listening to the context.

The process may look something like the following. The pioneers begin by engaging in 360-degree listening that includes attention to God, the context, the Christian tradition and contemporary Christian partners. This 360-degree listening will require the pioneer to develop a substantial rhythm of prayer, a deep immersion in the Christian tradition and an ongoing dialogue with a range of Christian partners who share a passion for mission. Engaging with the context requires that pioneers are *present* in the context. If the pioneers don't live in the area in which a fresh expression is envisaged, some or all of them may consider moving. (If pioneers are prepared to consider parachuting into a context for a weekly service but not to identify with local people by actually living alongside them, they may care to reflect on the depth of their commitment to establishing a viable fresh expression in that particular context). Prayerful, partnered presence in the context will:

- facilitate a more authentic grasp of the needs of the local community;
- lead to a better understanding of how to respond to these needs;
- give rise to humility and love;
- allow the pioneers to work towards the creation of a receptive environment for a fresh expression;
- help them in the timing of launching a fresh expression;
- allow them to maintain a clear focus on the task in hand;
- make commitment for the long haul more likely.

Each of the headings in this chapter represents a part of the process of active, prayerful attention to the context. In this multifaceted and highly integrated approach to pioneering, 'getting started' isn't something that happens after a vision has been generated. Since the approach to pioneering a fresh expression outlined here is rooted in love and involves prayerful immersion in the context, getting started is highly likely to happen along the way. To put it simply, this approach deliberately avoids working things out carefully in advance and then moving to an action phase in which the pioneers seek to put their well-rounded vision into practice. Although there may be a distinct point at which a fresh expression is 'launched', the assumption here is that vision will emerge out of the attentive and prayerful activity of the pioneers (note the plural!) in situ.

## Listening

### Prayer

The great Methodist pioneer, John Wesley, wrote: 'God does nothing except in response to believing prayer.' Prayer is the beginning, middle and end of all that the Christian thinks, says and does. A fresh expression emerges and grows out of prayer. It will be planted in prayer, rooted in prayer, growing in prayer and bearing fruit in prayer. If you are a pioneer or stakeholder involved in discerning the beginnings of a vision for a fresh expression, I would encourage you to ask the following questions:

- Are you praying?
- How long have you been praying about this?
- Have you considered adopting fasting as an aid to your prayerful discernment?
- What have you felt God is saying to you at each stage about the vision?
- How are you discerning God's voice?
- Who is discerning this with you?
- Who else is praying about this?
- Who is committed to praying for you and with you?
- Are you getting out and praying on the streets in and around the area in which the fresh expression is envisaged?
- If not, why not?
- What is the spiritual history of the place in which you hope to plant a church?

If you don't know the answer to the last point, it might be worth doing some research to find out about God's activity in this area over the centuries. This will often turn up interesting examples of previous mission activity that may offer useful insights or lessons for your own efforts. It may also provide a helpful background for any issues or problems that your process of discernment has uncovered – helping to explain why things are as they are in the present.

## Listening

'Absolutely unmixed attention is prayer.'[1] So wrote the theologian and political activist Simone Weil. Just as pioneers must root the vision for a fresh expression of Church in attention to God (in prayer), so they must also root it in attention to their context. If you are a pioneer you will be listening to your context. Patience is key here. Listening properly and hearing more than snippets takes a long time. Pioneers need to be prepared to listen long and hard and in a variety of places in order to hear as much as possible. This is also where the importance of collaboration becomes apparent. The more pioneers who are listening, the more they will hear! As pioneers listen alongside others, they will be able to ensure that they are hearing correctly: balancing and informing one another's perception of what is heard. Of course, listening in this sense is not just done with the ears. Listening in the sense in which we are speaking will be multi-layered. Deep listening involves researching the context on the internet and in libraries. It means interacting with local shops, businesses and service-providers, and engaging with local authorities, councillors, the police, social workers, community groups, schools, healthcare centres and the local people themselves. This broad interaction is crucial if the pioneers are to get a firm grasp on the nature and shape of the context – a grasp that includes what is apparent on the surface as well as the systems and ways of being that are not quite so obvious at first sight: the taken for granted habits or the things that are kept out of sight but that deeply affect for good or ill the daily lives of those living in the context. Chapter 4 offered the example of the pioneer Alex Smeed, who engaged in

---

1 S. Miles (ed.), *Simone Weil: An Anthology*, London: Penguin, 2005, p. 232.

an 18-month mission audit of his context in Glasgow in order to understand the area and its history. This type of activity will make a radical difference to the pioneers and will result in a far higher possibility of the fresh expression connecting on a deep level with those who live and work in a particular area.

## Presence

To listen to a context, pioneers must be physically present. It is not possible to develop a vision for a fresh expression in the comfort of a vicarage study or from outside an area looking in. Chapter 4 drew on the lovely insight from Angela Shier-Jones that 'Pioneering ministry cannot be done to a community by someone who knows what they need, it can only be done with a community by someone who shares their need.'[2] I have repeated the quote here because the principle is of critical importance. In spite of this, it is often overlooked. Pioneers who sense a call from God to develop a vision for a fresh expression in a particular place need to know and love that place, which can only happen if they are present – sharing in the lives and needs of those they seek to serve. If they don't live in the context they should consider why, and whether it is desirable and indeed feasible to move. If you are the pioneer it may be that you already live in the area, but it will be important to ask yourself how embedded you are. In other words, are you *really* present? How well are you integrated into the area? How well do you know local people and businesses? Are you aware of the particular concerns? If the answer to these questions is generally in the negative, how might you change your lifestyle patterns to be more present? If you have taken a decision to move into an area, have you really counted the cost? What are the implications for you and your family? Are you prepared to send your children to the local school, for example? If you are remaining outside an area and travelling in for services and events, have you weighed

---

2 A. Shier-Jones, *Pioneer Ministry and Fresh Expressions of Church*, London: SPCK, 2009, p. 123.

the impact of this? What effect might this detachment have on your vision, the message of the gospel and the way it is received?

## Humility

As they set about the work of planting a fresh expression, pioneers must emulate the example of Jesus, who explained to his disciples that, 'the Son of Man did not come to be served, but to serve' (Mark 10.45 NIV).

The need for humility was discussed in Chapter 4. I raise it again here simply to underline the fact that this is a crucial virtue for pioneers to develop. In essence, virtues are habits that shape our characters as we practise them. The more attention we devote to the practice of a particular habit, the greater its impact on our character. As pioneers set about generating a vision for a fresh expression, it will be important for them to consider devoting particular attention to growing in humility. Humility will enable the pioneer to engage in genuine listening but it will also help them to learn from their mistakes without fear of embarrassment, and to examine their motives for getting involved in a pioneering project in the first place. Most importantly of all, it will mean that the pioneer is able to follow Jesus' own example and set about being the servant of all in order to witness to God's abundant love. As the wider Church witnesses pioneers operating in genuine humility, there will be a far greater chance of creative, respectful dialogue and the accompanying possibility of cross-fertilization and the mutual learning of important lessons.

## Envisioning

### Understanding the need

It is relatively easy to sit in a church office or coffee shop with one or two enthusiastic others, imagine what a particular area or context might need (or enjoy), and then put together an exciting-sounding vision for a fresh expression – all pre-packaged and ready to drop into place. I know this because I've been guilty of it – and I've seen lots of others do it too. Unfortunately it happens and continues to happen in churches all over the UK. I would like to say that it is motivated by the best intentions, but at best the motives are often mixed: a combination of a desire to get more people involved with a particular church's programme and a failure to get out into the wider community and understand what's actually needed.

The thing is, people don't need to come to the church's new event. I know this because churches have been adopting this approach for many years without widespread success. Of course, I meet fellow Christians who enthusiastically tell me about their latest church event – they may even call it a fresh expression – that pulled in hundreds of people. But behind the apparent success of drawing in a large crowd is a deeper set of questions relating to how such events help to create and shape disciples of Jesus, and whether the tens of thousands of people in that particular town or city who didn't come along will ever have the opportunity to meet the Jesus of the everyday – the Jesus who is with us in the school-run and the worries about paying the bills, as well as at a highly produced church event. People are not absent from church because it's at an inconvenient time or in a 'churchy' space, or because the music isn't right or the sermon doesn't have enough video clips. Church-folks allow themselves to imagine that this is true because changing *these* things is relatively easy. I'm sure, if asked, people would give myriad answers to the question of why they're not in church. I'd like to suggest that one of the biggest reasons is because they don't know that you and I love them. If I know someone loves me I will go along to almost anything with them. And if, when I get there, I meet others who clearly love each other and welcome me in love, I'll want to stick around. I can honestly say that I wouldn't mind what we sat on – it could be pews, the floor or sofas. And I reckon I could take the long words and confusing concepts in my stride because – since I'd sense the love – I would guess that they did all of this for good reason, and that the things that went on had something to do with the love, and that sooner or later I'd be helped to understand it all for myself.

So if my friend loves me and asks me to come along to church, I'll come. But if my friend invites me to something because its their church's new event and the pastor is hoping it will be well attended and has told everyone to ask their friends, I won't come. Or I might come once, so that my friend doesn't feel bad, but I won't come again because why on earth would I? They haven't shown me that they love me and it has cost them exactly nothing. The thing that makes the church worth bothering to be a part of is love – outrageous love. Demonstrating love isn't easy. It takes time and there may be no obvious results. Love is messy and might mean that the church has to do a whole heap of things it would rather not. But there it is – there's no alternative.

A fresh expression might therefore host an event, but the event must be a loving response to genuine need. To find out what the genuine needs of a community are, the people of God have to get out and about, get their hands dirty. Sara Savage reminds us about the importance of listening in the task of sharing the gospel: 'The experience of being listened to is so close to the experience of being loved as to be indistinguishable.'[3] If you're a pioneer developing a vision for a fresh expression, it's essential that you consistently ask yourself what the most pressing need on the ground is. You'll discover this by walking, looking, talking and listening to lots of people. If, while you're trying to discern your vision, you realize that you've misjudged local needs, it will be important for you to be holding things lightly enough to change tack and take an alternative approach. Once the need and a potential response are discerned, pioneers must plan an approach that ultimately empowers those whose needs they are seeking to meet, rather than simply serving in a way that encourages dependency. Jesus came to seek and to save the lost, and he calls all Christians – including pioneers – to go out in love and do likewise. Genuine love will propel pioneers out with a desire to be of genuine service and to help meet the tidal wave of need. In doing this pioneers will be acting as faithful disciples and their efforts will bear fruit – fruit that will last.

---

3 S. Savage, Beta Course, session 2; see www.betacourse.org.

## The vision

A fresh expression will emerge from a vision. The vision may begin with one person or a small group. It may emerge as a result of discernment by a parish, a deanery, a diocese, a circuit, a synod or a network. However it emerges, there will be some key questions to ask – and answer – if the vision is to flourish and result in the emergence of a healthy and sustainable fresh expression.

At the risk of stating the obvious, the first question is: What exactly *is* the vision, and can it be summed up in fairly simple terms? It should be concise enough to provide something reasonably clear for the initial stakeholders to begin to work towards, but not so tightly defined that it squeezes out any possibility of organic evolution as the Spirit leads and as new people join in.

Second, to whom does the vision really belong? It's very important for stakeholders to place all of their cards face-up on the table at this point. It may be fine for the initial vision to belong to an individual, but motives have to be declared and examined and the vision must quickly be owned more widely.

Third, what is at the root of the vision? There are many reasons for starting a fresh expression. Some are less commendable than others. It's relatively easy to make a new idea sound appealing and 'sell' it to others by tapping into their hopes and fears. Love must be at the root of any vision to start a fresh expression – love and nothing else. Other motives will lead to a lot of wasted time and money and a great deal of disappointment. If love isn't there, the pioneers should ask God to give them a new vision that *is* rooted in love. Idealized notions of community are especially destructive. In *Life Together*, Dietrich Bonhoeffer issues a clear warning to those who are tempted to work towards an idealized version of Christian community:

> Innumerable times a whole Christian community has broken down because it has sprung from a wish dream. Every human wish dream that is injected into the Christian community is a hindrance to genuine community and must be banished if genuine community is to survive. He who loves his dream of

community more than the Christian community itself becomes the destroyer of the latter.[4]

Related to this last point is the question: 'By what process was the vision developed?' A sound process for vision development will involve prayer, discernment, consultation, deep listening and patience among other things.

## Focus

Developing a vision through prayerful listening – and planting a fresh expression over months and years – requires the ability to focus. Pioneers whose attention is distracted by a range of responsibilities elsewhere will be less effective in planting a fresh expression. If you're a minister with other responsibilities but who also senses a call to pioneering, you'll clearly have to weigh the amount of time you're likely to be able to give to a new venture very carefully. If your current responsibilities are wide-ranging and non-negotiable, might it be possible for a new community to emerge under the leadership or guidance of a group of others? Perhaps this is a valuable opportunity for the releasing and enabling of those within your pastoral care. Whether or not you're already in full-time church leadership, if you're keen to begin developing a vision for pioneering a fresh expression, you'll need to be honest about your current responsibilities. What else is going on in your life? Do work and/or family commitments mean that taking on something else is going to lead to added strain? Are you able to give the fresh expression the time, energy and focus that are necessary? Who and what will you particularly focus on in the early stages and how might this evolve as the fresh expression takes root and flourishes? If your answer is 'everyone and everything', you'll need to rethink and find a more realistic, sustainable and Christ-like approach. How will you decide what and who to focus on? How will you monitor this? To whom will you be accountable as regards your focus? Many pioneers develop a

---

4 D. Bonhoeffer, *Life Together*, London: SCM Press, 1954, p. 15.

'council of reference' to help with accountability on a range of issues, not least managing the balance between pioneering and the rest of life. A council of reference is a small group of trusted individuals – at least some of whom don't have a direct stake in the fresh expression – who meet regularly to provide encouragement, wisdom, perspective and prayer support. A group like this will be most effective and valuable if it begins to meet in the early stages of the project. This way – members are inside the story from the outset and more likely to have a clarity unclouded by the pioneers' version of events.

## Resourcing

### Commitment

Fresh expressions take years and even decades to plant, establish and reach the point at which they bear fruit. Pioneering a fresh expression is a wonderful privilege as well as a call to a sacrificial lifestyle. Of course, all who follow Jesus are called to count the cost and to die to self. But the call to pioneer has particular costs of its own. As Chapter 4 showed, if you're a pioneer contemplating a vision for a fresh expression, it's vital that you and others involved count the likely cost very early on. That cost will be in terms of both how many years you may have to spend tending to the fresh expression, as well as how much of your life is likely to be affected. Be brutally honest with yourself and your co-workers about what is likely to be required as the emerging vision for a fresh expression begins to come to life. Are you and your family prepared to put in years or even decades in a particular place? Are you and your loved ones able to put aside other possible futures in favour of *this* future? Are you willing to open your home and be available to those around you?

It's also important to find out the extent to which various stakeholders are committed. Are you aware of what it is that they expect in return for their commitment? Can you meet these expectations? How might the emerging community encourage deeper commitment from others as things get underway?

As pioneers attend to the various facets set out above, they will be preparing fertile ground in which a realistic and healthy vision for a fresh expression might be planted and nurtured.

## Collaboration

In one of their helpful Share guides on fresh expressions and pioneer ministry, Michael Moynagh and Andy Freeman write: 'It is time to think less about pioneers and more about pioneering teams.'[5] This is really important but it is only the beginning. As well as working in a team to get the initial vision off the ground, pioneers need to think about the entire venture in collaborative terms.

The desire to pioneer any fresh expression arises out of a God-given longing to create opportunities for as many people as possible to find a home in the community of God's people. The Christian life is a call to community: we love and worship and strive *together*. Pioneers collaborate with one another, with God *and* those with whom they are called to serve and minister. Since collaboration is a mark of a mature expression of Christian community, then it must be an integral part of the DNA of any pioneering work from the start. To ensure that this happens, pioneers must avoid the temptation of trying to be gifted at everything. The initial pioneers may well possess multiple talents but their call is to release the gifts that God has given others. So if you're a pioneer considering a vision for a fresh expression, you'll need to ask yourself: With whom has the vision been shaped? Does it need to be more widely shared so that others might help shape it? Collaboration doesn't mean the absence of a leader, but leadership must be accountable, shared where possible and monitored at every stage. As you ponder the question of leadership, you might like to ask whether it's possible to have revolving leadership,[6] dif-

5 M. Moynagh and A. Freeman, *How Should we Start?*, Fresh Expressions, Share Booklet 2, 2011, p. 6.

6 For more on revolving leadership, see J. Myers, *Organic Community: Creating a Place Where People Naturally* Connect, Grand Rapids: Baker Books, 2007. On healthy leadership in fresh expressions, see also S. Savage and E. Boyd-Macmillan,

ferent people leading on different aspects of the initiative according to their various gifts. Collaboration relies on people pulling together and communicating clearly about what they're willing and able to bring to the initiative. It will be important for those involved to understand the various limitations on others so that bitterness and resentment don't set in as some feel they're carrying the greater part of the load or being taken for granted. The pioneers in the initial team and, in time, the emerging community need to develop the habit of having frank and honest conversations about the time and resources each is able to bring to the initiative. Pioneers might also ask themselves:

- Is there scope for the initial team to grow numerically?
- What happens if team members quit – is the initiative still sustainable?
- Are commitments from certain members time-limited – that is, can you build with a temporary team or are long-termers needed?
- How will the team – and emerging community – keep the energy levels up and the vision alive, especially once the initial euphoria and high expectations have receded a little?
- How will the initial team and the emerging community deal with disagreements and differences of opinion?

Among other things, collaboration requires clear understanding of shared goals and aims and willingness on the part of those involved to be vulnerable. Jean Vanier addresses both of these points in his excellent book, *Community and Growth*. He writes:

> People come together in community because they want to create a place of caring. Community is not for producing things outside of itself; it is not a gathering of people struggling to win a cause. It is a place of communion where people care for others, and are cared for by others; a place where they become vulnerable to one another.[7]

---

*The Human Face of the Church: A Social Psychology and Pastoral Theology Resource for Pioneer and Traditional Ministry*, Norwich: Canterbury Press, 2007.

7 J. Vanier, *Community and Growth*, London: Darton, Longman & Todd, 1979.

Pioneers collaborate with God, one another and those whom they seek to serve to create something beautiful. Not in order to construct a utopian ideal but to enable genuine community – with all its challenges and benefits – to emerge. Nurturing a spirit of collaboration from the outset will mean that the fresh expression that gradually emerges will be a place where people are able to find a genuine welcome and a life-giving opportunity for communion and intimacy; a place they're given permission to contribute their God-given gifts – not for the sake of 'growth' or some other worthy-sounding purpose, but in love and for the good of all.

## Wider support

Alongside the development of the initial – and ongoing – vision, pioneering a fresh expression requires wider support. As far as is reasonably possible it should be undertaken with the goodwill, blessing and prayer support of other local churches or networks. It is likely, or at least possible, that those able to offer support for a new initiative will also be involved in the formation of the vision and the provision of necessary resources. The following questions will be helpful as the groundwork gets underway:

1 What kind of support is required? The list will always begin with prayer and is likely to also include financial support, ongoing encouragement, introductions to significant gatekeepers and general good will.
2 Where will the pioneers go to get this support? Who are the relevant gatekeepers and permission-givers? Who else might be willing to get on board with the project? There may be a number of local 'people of peace' willing to offer various kinds of support if made aware of the project. How might the pioneers find out who and where these people are and communicate their vision to generate support?
3 For how long will support be required? Prayer support is perhaps more easily guaranteed than ongoing financial support. A realistic idea of time frame will be helpful when approaching potential supporters.

4  It is important for the pioneers and supporters to be clear about one another's expectations. Are supporters happy to part with resources, financial or otherwise, with no more than their best wishes for the success of the new venture? If they are expecting something in return, or a particular outcome – perhaps one that benefits their own work, cause or agenda – are the pioneers willing and able to meet these expectations?

## Available resources

Establishing a fresh expression will require resources. A significant part of the groundwork, therefore, is establishing what these are likely to be and whether it's going to be possible to procure and sustain them. Resources in this context fall under three basic headings: human, spatial and financial. The simplest, home-based, low-tech, organic community needs *people* who are prepared to give time and energy, a *place* to meet (even if that's just a living room), and at least a little *money*, even if it's only to buy food so that the emerging community can gather around a table and share a meal. Whether the vision for the fresh expression is large or small, the pioneers and stakeholders will need to ask themselves what resources will be required in the early stages and how this might be likely to change as the fresh expression grows. They will need to establish whether getting these resources is possible and if not, they'll have to go back to God and seek clarification. Once the pioneers have established what resources are required, they need to be clear about the length of time they're likely to be available. If the resources offered at the early stages are time-limited, how will the pioneers ensure that a plan for procuring fresh ones is built into the wider vision?

I asked my research group to offer their thoughts on the key factors in undertaking the groundwork for the establishment of a fresh expression. Their responses follow. If you are prayerfully considering pioneering a fresh expression, I hope the comments will shape your own reflections on what first steps might be necessary.

## Comment feed

> Responses to the question: 'What is key in the groundwork
> for a fresh expression?'

## Sue Wallace

Prayer. Taking time to listen to God and to the people we meet
around us. A willingness to try something and admit that we are
learning as we go along.

## Steve Clarke

Listening – to God and the locality: people; communities; buildings; culture and history. God's heart and eyes for a place or
culture: people will see straight through you if you don't love them
or they know they are a 'project'. Gathering a team prepared to
'tabernacle' (move into the neighbourhood) is the way to go about
things. Jesus sent people out in teams. Going it alone is lonely and
the temptation is to pull people in who are de-churched, because
we long for and are wired for 'team'. I think this hinders the long-
term missional focus of a community. Whereas a strategically
gathered team can have in it a mission DNA from the outset. But
I guess any team carries with it an already defined culture that will
shape a church, so there are disadvantages to this approach.

## Robert Warren

Don't lose sight of the gospel as countercultural.

## Ned Lunn

Prayer. Praying individually, passionately seeking God in your life, praying corporately, passionately seeking God within a community, allowing collective discernment, eagerly awaiting the Spirit to speak through others. Watching for God already moving and not guessing where he might move in the future. If you can't see or hear God in the present, you have little chance of seeing or hearing him in the future.

## Mark Berry

Pioneering always begins with observation, reading the landscape, looking for the opportunities and listening to the Spirit. We took Luke 10 very seriously – Jesus sent the disciples out in small groups to offer peace to households – we began by asking the questions: 'Where are the communities in need of peace? Where are the households?' We tried to identify the hubs and find out where to knock. The notion of 'the people of peace' has become commonplace recently and there is a reason for that. We spoke directly to key people, leaders, gatekeepers face to face, in their places, and simply asked: 'What would peace look like/mean for you and your community?' And then we offered that to them. The crucial thing for us is that we have no desire to pull people out of their communities and into ours. We stay in their communities as guests – sharing our lives in the heart of their community. We don't see our mission as growing our community/church but as exposing people to the loving, living God in the way we live with them long-term. So we focus and work hard on our community: the way we breathe prayer for each other; the way we enable real intimacy and live transparently with each other; the way we uphold and sustain each other socially and spiritually to live an embedded faith.

## Jonny Baker

Listening, imagination, and discerning the Spirit – none of these are easy things.

## John Drane

Prayer, discernment, self-awareness among those involved – of their own strengths and weaknesses, as well as their own spiritual journeys.

## Joe Knight

Prayer, prayer and more prayer. Also spending time getting to know your environment: drinking lots of coffee with local people, church leaders of all denominations, neighbours, shop workers, councillors and even Members of Parliament is vital. Making friends is key. Establishing a strategy, or at least some initial steps for establishing a seedbed for shared vision and values, is ideal for nurturing an embryonic community. But prayer is the most important factor: personal prayer and prayer with others. We must also have the courage to become the answer to our prayers. Prayer essentially roots us in God and propels us into his mission, enabling us to grow genuine relationships with others in the context and to build Christ-centred communities. Only in the place of prayer can everything else begin and only in the place of prayer can it truly flourish.

## Jo Cox

Team, vision, understanding expectations, recognition of the length of time that developing a fresh expression is likely to take (many years not a few months), realism about the costs involved – financial, psychological, ecclesiastical.

## Ian Meredith

Relationships. Be real about forming them with folk in the neighbourhood, not just a clique of Christians. Pray and let the Holy Spirit lead. Don't just do stuff and hope the Spirit catches up with you!

## Janet Webb

Prayer, discernment, freedom to explore, release from the institution, spending time with non-Christians and understanding them. Understand how the secular community works where you are by immersing yourself in it.

## Ellen Louden

I think one of the basic tasks is to find out whether a fresh expression is actually the right thing. If there is something that already exists in the location then, rather than starting something new, perhaps the existing initiative might be enhanced? If there is real need and this can be discerned in a tangible way, then the next move might be to discover who within that locale or interest group will be the pioneer(s). I think it is always best if this sort of thing emerges from a ground level of 'need' rather than from above. What I mean is that I'm not sure that a vicar or bishop or other keen person thinking it might be a nice idea to start a café church in such-and-such a high street because that sounds like a good idea, is really the best way to get authentic community going. So research the area, find key local people who might be the foundation of a project and start small – that would be the key groundwork.

## Chris Howson

The groundwork for a fresh expression is in recognizing the context that you are to be based in. What are the concrete needs of a community? Who has been marginalized and needs their voice to be heard? What groups of people have local churches failed to engage with? To find all this out, it is worth doing some serious community research into your locality. Even if you think you know an area pretty well, you may be quite surprised at the impact of small changes in demographics. Go to local libraries, look up local government information websites, read the local paper, and go and talk to people that you haven't listened to before.

## Bishop Mark Bryant

The beginning of the vision for a fresh expression may well come from a strong intuitive sense by a Christian that there is a particular group of people with whom they feel called to work, or a particular community in which they feel called to work. Beyond this (prayerful) intuition, the key groundwork is taking time to get to know people, and to get to know the community.

## Bishop John Went

Identifying a group of people who have a heart to reach a group of people (in a geographical area or a network) who are unreached at present with the gospel; then undertaking some kind of audit to identify the exact identity of such a group and what their needs might be, and beginning to build bridges into that community. Double listening: to others and to God. Identify a team with the gifts to sustain the life of a fresh expression and practical questions, such as where to meet and how often.

## Beth Keith

Understanding and being part of the context, imagining what could develop, vocalizing a vision for something new, building a team suited to the context, vision and resources available, establishing lightweight and robust accountability structures. Long-term and short-term planning is helpful, but over-planning is not a good idea. However, some fresh expressions start without any prior official planning. Making the most of these opportunities may require extra support and flexibility based on the specific circumstances. These new churches, which appear to grow naturally, can yield some of the most surprising and encouraging developments.

## Ben Norton

Listening! It is so important that the fresh expression is incarnational rather than a programme that is planted because it has worked elsewhere. If an inherited church is struggling it has more than likely lost contact with the people it is trying to reach. Listening to the needs of the community or sub-culture you are trying to reach will teach you much more than putting something on that people might like to come to. It will also force you to think about what it is you are doing and why! If you go in and plant a church that looks really cool and attractive you will not face the real issues of ecclesiology that people want answered. Such as why do we have to worship rather than why do we have to worship in 'this' way . . .

## Ben Edson

An attentive spirit is the crucial groundwork. Listen to God and be patient. Don't rush for success but nurture relationships at the beginning that will sustain the fresh expression and the pioneers in the long term. While you have the time, use it wisely, listening to God and growing your embryonic pioneering community.

## Chris Neal

The following must be in place as foundational: a sense of calling, passion and vision all given in and through the power of God's Spirit; a willingness to pray for the people of peace who will be part of the founding community – whether as the 'stranger' who feels called to a particular context, or those who already inhabit the context; building a common sense of purpose and vision, informed and shaped by agreed values that are not simply espoused but also become embodied within the community; a willingness to be patient as the culture and context are mapped and understood; in the light of the mapping, a willingness to explore what missional living might look like within that context – this will allow the Spirit to show and develop models and life-styles, rather than imposing a previously worked model; a deep commitment to prayer and a rhythm of life that informs and shapes the developing community; openness and a willingness to explore an expression of Christian Community that is not shaped by any previous maps.

## Ian Bell

It is essential that before a fresh expression is formed there is intentional, patient and prayerful discernment of the context. If mission is truly about discovering the activity of God and joining in what God is doing, then it follows that this period of spiritual discernment is indispensable. Patience in this process is vital, though sometimes difficult because of the expectation of speedy visible results – either self-imposed or placed on the pioneer by others. Prayerful discernment takes time, and rushing this element of the process is counterproductive, as vital clues to God's activity and future direction may easily be missed. The pioneer's familiarity with the context will vary from one situation to another but, in all cases, it is important to be attentive to that context and develop the best possible understanding of it. Interrogating and rehearsing the narrative of the context in which a pioneer is working is essential to the development of a fresh expression that is contextually suited. It is tempting to hasten this process, but the likelihood is that time saved at this stage may result in a disproportionate amount being consumed later, when mistakes need to be rectified or a different direction taken. Another key element of necessary groundwork is the development of adequate ownership by potential stakeholders – other local Christian groups and individuals, permission-givers within denominational structures, management and oversight groups, and people in the community where the fresh expression is to be formed. Some indication of the availability of resources is useful, though there is a delicate balance to be struck between prudent planning and a venture of faith! Jesus warns against a safe but unimaginative approach to mission on the one hand (the parable of the talents, Luke 19.12–28), and against unthinking recklessness on the other (the parable of the tower, Luke 14.28–9). Somehow the pioneer needs to achieve a balance, with sufficient vision, knowledge and resources to make it a potentially viable enterprise, without seeking to keep everything on hold until every last detail is in place. If there is a continuum that has complete inertia at one end and entire recklessness at the other, the pioneer is likely to be found nearer – though not too near – the latter. So some practical building blocks need to be in place or assured, but only sufficient that the element of faith venture or holy risk is not removed or diluted.

## Further reading

Bonhoeffer, D., *Life Together*, London: SCM Press, 1954.

Chew, M. and Ireland, M., *How to do Mission Action Planning: A Vision-Centered Approach*, London: SPCK, 2009.

Male, D. (ed.), *Pioneers for Life: Explorations in Theology and Wisdom for Pioneering Leaders*, Oxford: Bible Reading Fellowship, 2011.

Moynagh, M. and Freeman, A., Share booklet 2: *How Should we Start?*, Fresh Expressions, 2011.

Myers, J.R. *Organic Community: Creating a Place Where People Naturally Connect*, Grand Rapids: Baker Books, 2007.

Rutba House, *Schools for Conversion: 12 Marks of a New Monasticism*, Eugene, OR: Cascade Books, 2005.

Savage, S. and Boyd-Macmillan, E., *The Human Face of the Church: A Social Psychology and Pastoral Theology Resource for Pioneer and Traditional Ministry*, Norwich: Canterbury Press, 2007.

Sine, T., *The New Conspirators: Creating the Future one Mustard Seed at a Time*, Downers Grove: InterVarsity Press, 2008.

Vanier, J., *Community and Growth*, London: Darton, Longmann & Todd, 2007.

Volland, M., *Through the Pilgrim Door: Pioneering a Fresh Expression of Church*, Eastbourne: Survivor, 2009.

# 7

# The Long Haul

## Introduction

Prior to taking up a teaching post in Durham, I worked as an ordained pioneer minister in the diocese of Gloucester. The issues on which I had to reflect, both in the earliest days of pioneering and as a fresh expression developed, form the backbone of this chapter.

One of the first things that I and those who appointed me needed to be clear about was the likely time frame for the project. The initial stakeholders – the diocese and I – had to decide whether we would focus on establishing a short-term, high impact, local initiative, or a long-term community with deep roots and a wide reach. Either of these – and any number of related alternatives – would have been entirely valid as a fresh expression.

Although the focus of this chapter is on sustaining pioneers and fresh expressions for the long haul, it is worth stating briefly that in a number of contexts it may be right to pioneer a fresh expression that is likely to have a relatively brief lifespan; a gathering that will enable those within a particular network to encounter Christ, grow as disciples and witness faithfully before moving on to be part of other Christian communities. This more fluid approach should not be adopted uncritically, and is not an endorsement of the aspects of Western culture that discourage or disable commitment. It is simply an acknowledgement that in certain situations, establishing a fresh expression that is likely to be temporary is the best way to enable people to encounter and engage with the gospel, and is therefore consistent with the missiological understanding of this book.

In Gloucester a number of considerations shaped our eventual decision to work towards establishing a fresh expression that would grow and flourish over a number of years. Questions about sustainability were necessary from the beginning but would also have been important if we had opted to facilitate an initiative that was deliberately seasonal.

In this chapter I focus on developing a sustainable approach to pioneering a fresh expression that assumes a commitment to the long haul. I've adopted a simple approach, addressing the pioneer directly in the first section of this chapter and factors relating specifically to the fresh expression in the second. In reality, of course, these two – the pioneer and the fresh expression – can only be considered separately with some difficulty. The health and shape of the one obviously affects those of the other. The need of the pioneer for spiritual sustenance, for example, will be met to some degree through the worshipping life of the emerging fresh expression, and the need for the fresh expression to be interlinked with a range of local churches and agencies will be at least partially facilitated by the activity of the pioneer. Having noted this, I begin by focusing on those things that the pioneer will address with energy and commitment if he or she is to be sustained for the long haul.

## Sustaining the pioneer

The areas I look at here are discussed under the headings of character, attention and care. I explain how I understand these, say something about why they deserve the pioneer's attention and suggest what she or he might do in each case.

### Character

In *Growing Leaders*, James Lawrence places enormous stress on the need for Christians to develop good character. Lawrence writes, 'Character is foundational to everything. You can be a gifted person, a talented leader, a natural enthusiast, an amazing speaker, but without godly character it all falls apart.'[1]

It's wrong to assume that this need to address character is more pressing for those in Christian leadership than Christians in general. If we follow this misguided logic we end up with an unrealistic expectation of leaders as holy supermen and women, while potentially adopting a more laid-back approach to our own characters. Clearly those who seek to follow Jesus must reject this approach and set their hearts and minds on developing godly character, not least because Jesus himself teaches his followers to 'Be perfect, therefore, as your heavenly Father is perfect' (Matt. 5.48). The main reason for particularly stressing character-issues in relation to those in Christian leadership is that if things fall apart for a Christian leader, the entire community in which they are involved feels the effects. This is likely to cause widespread and long-lasting damage, and it's therefore important that those in leadership address character issues as a matter of the highest priority and continue to do so throughout their lives.

So far what I have said applies to all Christians – and therefore to all those in Christian leadership. But what of pioneers? Is there a sense in which pioneers might need to pay closer attention to particular aspects of their characters as they set about planting fresh expressions that are to be sustainable over the long haul?

The answer is both no and yes. As I have already pointed out, *all* those who follow Jesus are, through the grace of the Father, to be open to the transforming power of the Holy Spirit who gently shapes our characters day by day so that we are 'conformed to the image of his Son' (Rom 8.29). In this sense pioneers are no different from any other Christians and should expect, like their fellow disciples, to manifest the fruit of the Spirit which is 'love, joy, peace, patience, kindness, goodness, faithfulness, gentleness and self control' (Gal. 5.22–3). For pioneers, the manifestation of this fruit will be the ability faithfully to enable an emerging fresh expression to engage in authentic worship and loving service.

---

1 J. Lawrence, *Growing Leaders: Reflections on Leadership, Life and Jesus*, Oxford: Bible Reading Fellowship, 2004, p. 123.

All Christian ministry, including pioneering, is demanding. What is particular to pioneering is the type of demand. For example, pioneering work – certainly in the early days – is likely to be lonely. To various extents the pioneer may face misunderstanding, disillusionment and discouragement. There will be pressure – real or imagined – to succeed, to generate an impressive work, quickly. This leads to any number of pitfalls, not least a destructive pride. And if this kind of success is sought but not forthcoming, the pioneer is likely to succumb to doubt, despair and a sense of personal failure. There are a number of mechanisms that pioneers might employ to cope with these difficulties. Some are healthy and life-enhancing, others – addictive or destructive behaviours – life-denying and diminishing. The character of the pioneer will be the deciding factor in enabling her or him to weather these storms and maintain physical, mental and spiritual health through the inevitable tough times.

If the character of the pioneer is to be conformed to that of Jesus Christ, then we must say something about what Jesus' character was like. When we consider Jesus as the Gospel writers witness to him, we recognize that what we are presented with is a *fully* human being. Here is a man of faultless love, truth, compassion, integrity and faithfulness. Here is the one who is able to forgive all and the one who came as the servant of all. The Jesus we encounter in the Gospels is to be the example for the pioneer. The pioneer will do well to meditate on the person and presence of Christ, seeking to encounter him and be transformed in the process. One who seeks to be sustained for the long haul will, with an open heart and outstretched hands, consistently seek the presence of the living Jesus in order to become a man or woman whose character is defined by love, truth, compassion, integrity and faithfulness. He or she will seek Jesus daily for the grace to be the servant of all and able to forgive all, and one who does these things will find both that he or she is sustained for the long haul and, since the character of Jesus is attractive, that others will be drawn in. As pioneers love and serve, encourage and forgive those with whom they are seeking to establish a fresh expression, people will be eager to collaborate with them in order to achieve something of lasting worth. I realize that there is a slight danger here of painting an idealistic picture, an image of the perfect pioneer who is more like a superhuman saint than a broken vessel. I make no apology for this. Following Jesus Christ is a high calling, and by the grace of God all who set out on this road can and should expect to be transformed in the very essence of their being so that they are more like him. Pioneering is a kind of calling within calling – a particular road that some of those who follow Jesus are given to walk. This road can be lonely and at times dangerous, but it is also a road on which high ideals and striving for godly perfection are not out of place. We walk, after all, with Jesus himself, and it is his presence with the pioneer that makes all the difference.

We have noted, then, that the character of the pioneer is of the utmost importance for the present and the future. The increasingly Christ-like character of the pioneer will enable the pioneer to be sustained for the long haul and effective in their pioneering work. We need to say a little more now about how that character is formed. It can be summed up in one deceptively simple word: attention.

## Attention

Attention to God through prayer, study of scripture, reception of the sacraments, corporate worship and acts of loving service have been recognized since the earliest days of the Church as parts of a whole that, when taken together, provide the means by which Christians are enabled to grow in holiness and be sustained through the joys and challenges of life. Pioneers do not need to start from scratch and reinvent the wheel when seeking to develop a mission spirituality that will sustain them for the long haul. There are abundant resources available to those who seek to thrive spiritually in Christian ministry.

The resources that have been handed to us through the various strands of the monastic traditions are receiving a great deal of attention at the moment. Many contemporary writers are outlining a new monasticism – a recovery or remembrance of aspects of monastic spiritual practice that might be valuable for those seeking to follow Christ and witness faithfully to him in the emerging Western culture. There is no doubt that some of this is a rather romanticized version of reality, but allowing for this there are certainly key insights and resources to be gained by the pioneer who engages with the work of writers on new monasticism.

At the heart of all monastic spirituality is the longing for union with God. All monastic practice is designed to fit this end and enable the followers of Jesus to fix their attention on him. Those things that distract from this goal are carefully avoided. Although it often conjures up an image of removal from the world to a life of cloistered isolation, in reality contemporary monastic practice and spirituality takes a variety of forms – many of which seek to enable attention to God amid the business of life rather than in quiet seclusion. A more helpful way to conceive of what is at the heart of these new monastic spiritualities is to imagine a simple rhythm of withdrawal and engagement – a model that the Gospel writers show Jesus adopting in order to be sustained in a demanding public ministry (the first chapter of Mark's Gospel provides a good example). Pioneers appropriating this model will make space daily, weekly, monthly and annually to fix their attention on God. These spaces for attention – ranging from minutes to days – will be created amid the pioneering work and will form the backbone of a rhythm of attention to God, to others and to self that will sustain the pioneer for the long haul.

In *Cave, Refectory, Road*, Ian Adams quotes Theophan the Recluse. He writes, 'There is nothing more important than prayer; therefore our greatest attention and most diligent attention must attend it.'[2] The pioneer takes this seriously and in withdrawal seeks to give full attention to God in prayer. It is here, in this place of encounter with the living God – this directing of the attention to the Love at the centre of creation – that the pioneer is nurtured, shaped, restored, energized and sent out to share the love of God. The work of the Christian is prayer, and it is in the place of prayer

2 I. Adams, *Cave, Refectory, Road: Monastic Rhythms for Contemporary Living*, Norwich: Canterbury Press, 2010, p. 50.

that the pioneer will be formed and sustained. It is as a result of prayer and nothing else that something worthwhile will emerge.

The resources offered at this time by new monasticism might be viewed as a gift of God. Of course, there are a variety of approaches for pioneers seeking to develop and maintain a robust mission spirituality. But many of the practices encouraged by new monasticism seem to be particularly suited to the nature of the task in which pioneers are currently called to engage. I invite the reader to investigate some of the books on the subject listed in Further Reading at the end of this chapter.

## Care

Effective pioneering work requires significant personal resources and mental, emotional, physical and spiritual energy. The pioneer who is properly cared for in these respects is more likely to be sustained for the long haul. By proper care I mean access from the outset to general and specific support, which will include maintaining deep and committed friendships, spending regular time with a mentor or coach, participating in a peer network and cultivating a life-giving sense of humour.

James Lawrence writes: 'Good friends are prepared to tell us the hard truths about us that we'd prefer not to hear, yet Christian leaders often find themselves without such close friendships . . . friends nurture us, encourage us and provide us with perspective.'[3] Pioneers cannot afford to be without friends. They will care for the pioneer even when she or he is tempted to put care for self at the bottom of the priority list. Putting in place time in which friendships can be forged *and* maintained will produce substantial dividends as the pioneering work goes forward.

### Friendships

Friendships will be both within the context but also, crucially, outside and away from the place in which the pioneer is facilitating

---

3 Lawrence, *Growing Leaders*, pp. 147–8.

a fresh expression. The opportunity to share openly and honestly about the delights as well as the challenges and difficulties inherent in pioneering is of huge importance. Pioneers will need to prioritize discerning which of their friendships are most suited to bearing the strain of sharing a long and often difficult road as a fresh expression gradually emerges. The friend who is able to walk the road with the pioneer will be one who is willing and able to listen, with whom the pioneer can laugh as well as cry, who refrains from being judgemental but has permission to be straight and to speak the difficult word where needed. Such a friend will be a source of encouragement and comfort. They will pray *for* the pioneer and *with* the pioneer. In sum, the pioneer will find him or herself sustained by a friend or friends whom God has gifted with the rare and beautiful combination of compassionate ears, the ability to offer wise counsel in due season and an intuitive understanding of when a comforting hug is the thing needed most.

## Mentoring and coaching

Recent research with pioneers has shown that those who have a mentor or coach are likely to be more effective in their pioneering work and more likely to sustain themselves for the long haul. Mentoring and coaching are processes that seek to enable the pioneer to achieve their potential and to weather the inevitable storms. They share a number of similarities but they are in fact distinct roles, and it will be useful for the pioneer to understand their own needs well enough to know which of the two is more suited to them.

In a traditional sense, mentoring will generally involve the pioneer spending time with an older and more experienced pioneer. The mentor will pass on their own knowledge and experience and may assist the less experienced pioneer in striving for opportunities that would otherwise have remained unimagined or out of reach.

A coach, on the other hand, does not necessarily have direct pioneering experience – although they might! – but will engage in particular processes with the pioneer that enable learning and development. The aim of these processes is that the pioneer become increasingly effective in carrying out his or her task. Mentoring and coaching are particularly helpful because of the unique contexts in which pioneers generally operate. However high the quality of their previous theological and practical training,[4] the nature of pioneering means that they are likely to encounter a range of situations and experiences for which they feel inadequately prepared. Regular time with a mentor or a coach will help the pioneer to work through unexpected or unusual situations, to learn from mistakes, maintain a positive focus and facilitate adaptations to the wider vision where necessary.

## Peer networks

If trusted friendships and good mentoring are essential for sustaining the pioneer for the long haul, so is membership of peer group or network. Pioneering can be exciting and rewarding but, as we have noted, it will inevitably involve the pioneer in negotiating challenge and difficulty. Loneliness is a common experience, as is misunderstanding, frustration, failure and even opposition. Gathering regularly with other pioneers will provide an essential forum for sharing stories of joy or difficulty, and for mutual learning, encouragement, advice and prayer. There are a number of examples of such networks at both local and national level. The Centre for Pioneer Learning in Cambridge, for example, aims 'to serve all pioneers who are establishing new forms of church and taking the church to new places throughout the UK and the world'.[5] Crucially, it aims to establish an environment where pioneers can learn together, seeking to resource lay and ordained pioneers and provide training, resources and support in a range of contexts.

---

4 This chapter assumes that the pioneer has undertaken some level of formal training prior to starting. This may range from the Mission-Shaped Ministry course – www.freshexpressions.org.uk/missionshapedministry – to a full-time degree at a theological college. The important thing is that a foundation has been put in place that will facilitate the pioneer's ongoing learning and theological reflection.

5 Taken from www.centreforpioneerlearning.org.uk.

VentureFX[6] is a bold pioneering ministry scheme that has been initiated by the Methodist Church to reach young adults who have no Christian heritage. It has sought to enable pioneers to facilitate projects nationwide and is already proving fruitful. From the outset the Methodist Church recognized and underlined the importance of the VentureFX pioneers' meeting together regularly as a peer network for mutual encouragement, support and training. Those involved are vocal about the importance of this regular opportunity for peer sharing and the positive impact it is having on their ministries.

In County Durham, where I am based, there are numerous ex-mining communities. In a number of these the Church has recognized the need for pioneering new forms of Church in order to engage with communities who have a range of social and spiritual needs. In partnership with a small number of others in an adjoining county, the possibility of collaborating on an inter-county network for pioneers in isolated ex-mining communities has recently been mooted. It is early days, but what is exciting is the recognition that the potential for establishing and supporting fresh expressions in challenging contexts is hugely increased by the possibility of pioneers committing to gather, share and pray together on a regular basis.

## A sense of humour

If pioneers are to be sustained for the long haul they need to be men and women who possess and regularly exercise a sense of humour. Pioneering is tough but it can also be fun. There will be lots to cry over but also much to laugh about. A sense of humour will keep the pioneer from taking themselves too seriously and will help them not to lose perspective.

The work in which pioneers engage is God's work, and while pioneers are co-workers, it is God who shoulders the greater part of the load. A sense of humour will ensure that pioneers are able to maintain a right assessment of themselves as co-workers rather

---

6 venturefxpioneer.blogspot.com.

than those on whom everyone and everything depends. It will also allow them to laugh at their own mistakes and failures – a habit that makes for a healthy soul, mind and body. And let's not forget that a sense of humour is attractive too! People are more likely to want to gather with pioneers who enjoy a good laugh and can share a joke than with those so absorbed in the seriousness of their task that they've forgotten their God-given capacity for humour. Robert Warren, a pioneer of many decades' experience, and part of my research group, continues to maintain a life-giving sense of humour. He provided the following response to one of the questions in my questionnaire: 'Pioneers shouldn't take themselves too seriously. Q: 'What is the difference between God and a Pioneer Leader?' A: 'God knows he is not a Pioneer Leader.'

## Sustaining the fresh expression

All the elements that I've set out above as necessary to sustain the pioneer over the long haul will also – with slight adjustments – be important for sustaining a fresh expression. Character, attention and care can and should be applied to the fresh expression itself. If it is to survive and thrive over the long haul, the new community will attend to its individual and corporate *character* – striving to become more like Jesus and recognizing the increasing presence of the fruit of the Spirit as evidence that this is happening. It will pay *attention* to God in prayer, in the study of scripture, in the celebration of the sacraments and in acts of loving service. It will also ensure that it takes good *care* of itself, investing in *friendships* both within and outside the community, seeking *mentors* to offer wise guidance on an uncertain road, being proactive in *networking* with other, similar communities either locally or nationally, and remembering each day the importance of a *sense of humour.* Giving time and attention to each of these will help sustain a fresh expression over the long haul. There are a number of other things to say, however.

In *Community and Growth*, Jean Vanier writes:

It is quite easy to found a community. There are always plenty of courageous people who want to be heroes, are ready to sleep on the floor, to work hard hours each day, to live in dilapidated houses. It's not hard to camp – anyone can rough it for a time. So the problem is not in getting the community started – there's always enough energy for take-off. The problem comes when we are in orbit and going round and round the same circuit. The problem is in living with brothers and sisters whom we have not chosen but who have been given to us, and in working ever more truthfully towards the goals of the community.[7]

Vanier goes on to explain that what he calls 'true community' implies a particular way of life and a commitment to seeing reality – rather than indulging in wish-dreams. According to Vanier, true community implies fidelity and forgiveness. He is clear that it's only possible when those involved have addressed the realities of communal life and are content with a God-given simplicity. He writes further:

A community is only being created when its members accept that they are not going to achieve great things, that they are not going to be heroes, but simply live each day with new hope . . . [8]

Vanier's perspective is deeply helpful as we consider how a new community, a fresh expression, might ensure from the start that it's geared up to be sustainable. It may start easily enough – in a flurry of energy and excitement, as Vanier points out above – but this initial energy and excitement will gradually, and quite naturally, dissipate, and if it is to survive, the emerging community must have at its heart a commitment to the reality of lives shared over the long haul.

---

7 J. Vanier, *Community and Growth*, London: Darton, Longman & Todd, 2007, pp. 108–9.

8 Vanier, *Community and Growth*, p. 109.

## Foundations

After the energy and excitement of the early months, the vision, goals and spirituality of the new community will gradually become clear and will need to be articulated and communicated. This is not just for the benefit of those within the fresh expression, since this doesn't just exist for itself but also for the wider community. By articulating its vision and goals, the new community gains an identity in the eyes of both the other local churches and the wider community. It begins to posses a shape, and the nature of its shared life and its particular calling will become clear to those around it. This process is an integral part of laying foundations.

As we consider the ways in which a fresh expression might ensure that it is sustainable, we must stress the importance of avoiding the temptation to overplan at the beginning. This is especially the case where the pioneer is being funded by the diocese, circuit, district or synod. Those entrusted with the stewardship of the church's financial resources quite naturally want to know how everything will pan out, what targets are in place, when things will happen, how many people will be involved and by what point the fresh expression might be paying its own way. The problem with lots of advance planning is that it tends to stifle opportunity for the Spirit of God freely to direct and shape the fresh expression. A fresh expression needs to be given a chance to emerge and live – to grow and flourish with the involvement of all those who join in before the vision becomes properly visible and targets are put in place. This understanding must be held in tension with the fact that for a community to be sustained over the long haul and for it really to thrive and flourish, there must come a time when the temptation (or desire) to be open to any new possibility and every new whim must be refused and goals and aims be clarified. Vanier is helpful again here:

> There is a time for everything; a time for conception, birth and growth. Then there is a time for reading what has been given and reflecting upon it. God gives us hearts so that we may be inspired by his Love and his Spirit, but he also gives us minds,

so that we may understand, clarify, discern and read what he is saying and giving in and through life.[9]

## Clarity

In contemporary Western culture the word community is used a great deal and can denote anything from sporadic membership of an online chat room to the school your children attend or the gym you wished you visited more often. Community has come to mean pretty much anything and, at times, almost nothing. We like the word because using it helps us feel that we're part of a group; that we're together with others. This desire is powerful and God-given. Many of us are members of a number of communities, some of which have a greater place in our hearts than others or engender a deep sense of worth and fulfilment. If we're not in any such community, or were once but are no longer, we may imagine that our deepest longing is for community. When pioneers set out to establish a fresh expression, they're often at least partially motivated by this desire to establish a community in which a shared need for togetherness and mutual support and affection can be realized. For the most part this is good and proper. After all, the good news of the gospel is that we are invited to step out of the poverty of our aloneness into membership of the community that is the people of God. But contemporary ideas about community – forged in the warping heat of a postmodern, individualistic, consumerist culture – can too easily become the enemy of true community. A fresh expression that seeks to be sustainable must enable those who join to achieve a right understanding of what community really is and of what it is not. Community is demanding. It's not simply being together with others on one's own terms. True community – community that's thriving and growing and life-giving – requires its members to be present on one another's terms. There is freedom but it's not the freedom only to take from the community to meet one's own perceived needs. The fresh expression that is seeking to make the long haul must lovingly help all the

---

9 Vanier, *Community and Growth*, p. 111.

members to grasp a firm understanding of the demands as well as the privileges of community.

## Sharing

A fresh expression that survives and thrives over a number of decades will be one that has learnt to share responsibility for everything that must be done. As I've stated previously, the Church doesn't need heroic pioneer leaders. Long-haul fresh expressions are begun by pioneers who work *with* others from day one, enabling and giving away responsibility with the clear intention of the fresh expression becoming self-sufficient and sustainable. In the early days the pioneer will make a concerted effort to draw out the best from those who join in, helping every member to exercise their gifts and encouraging them over and over until they're clear that what they have to bring is valuable and welcome. Fresh expressions that thrive over the long haul are those in which the voices of all who are involved are heard frequently. These communities have recognized that ongoing and in-depth discussion of what to do and how to do it is essential. To ensure that this is the habit of the community, pioneers must focus on enabling it from the earliest days. They will need to be patient and to facilitate spaces in which all the members of the emerging fresh expression have the opportunity to be heard. The temptation to set out the impassioned top-down vision must be avoided, and the truth in relation to each new situation or challenge must be allowed to emerge from the discussion of the group. The newest and youngest members should be given the opportunity to speak and their opinions given equal weight. A community that gives its members permission to speak will be one in which tough questions are heard and various tensions given the opportunity to surface. This is important and will contribute to sustainability. Tough questions exist in a community, whether members feel able to articulate them or not. A community that's unafraid of addressing the difficult questions that life and faith throw up will become a strong one in which members feel they're able to be themselves without fear. Likewise, when tensions arise, a community that embraces these as a natural and inevitable part of life, giving time and energy to seek resolution, will be one where members are deeply invested and in which they're able to grow towards becoming more fully human in truth and love.

## Limitations

As a new fresh expression takes root it may seek to be involved in a wide range of social and spiritual activities in and around its local area, even perhaps nationally or, in time, internationally. The fresh expression that thrives over the long haul will be one that exercises wisdom about the extent to which it's able to be involved in a range of outside activities. Some fresh expressions emerge in response to a very clear need, and in such cases the focus is clear from the start and will help members to concentrate their energies in a way that is sustainable. In other cases, such as where there is lots of local need, there will be a temptation for the members to try to respond to as much as possible. It's in contexts like this that the community will need to exercise corporate discernment and perhaps even bring in a wise guide who is able to assist in making clear decisions about what's possible given the resources available.

## Interdependence

A sustainable fresh expression will be one that's invested in creating and maintaining strong partnerships with other churches and the wider community. The fresh expression that is outward facing, eager to collaborate with those around them who share common aims, will find that as the years pass they become recognized as having something valuable to contribute. Members will be called upon to take part in initiatives that are considered to be widely important. This will be particularly apparent when local or regional events take a turn for the worse and the local community instinctively turns to the members of the fresh expression for help and support.

In this chapter we've considered some of the factors that will sustain pioneers and fresh expressions over the long haul. Doubtless there are many more we could add to the list. As we've stressed throughout this book, the key thing for pioneers and all involved in planting and growing fresh expressions to remember is that this is first and foremost God's work, and in his great mercy he involves us in the task. As we work with God in pioneering new forms of Church, the words of Jesus to his disciples with which I concluded Chapter 5 will once again be worth holding on to: 'I am the vine; you are the branches. If you remain in me and I in you, you will bear much fruit; apart from me you can do nothing' (John 15.5 NIV).

## Comment feed

> Responses to the question: 'What advice would you offer pioneers about sustaining themselves and a fresh expression for the long haul?'

### Ben Edson

Die to self. Give up that which you want the church to be and let the community be what it senses God is calling it to be. The pioneer is the servant of the Church. Never forget this and don't become so egocentric that you think that you are the centre. Christ is the centre of the Church and you are called to serve both him and his Church. Rant over . . .

### Ben Norton

Get used to frustration, growth is slow and it can be a lonely place to be because you never feel as though you fit anywhere. At times there is nothing to rely upon other than the Holy Spirit. Be brave and go out. You might never come back, but that's OK.

## Beth Keith

I'm obviously going to mention the importance of team, support from your denomination, mentoring and getting your finances in order. But alongside all that I'd say that regular tea and cake with wise friends will sustain a pioneer. Why? Because pioneering something new is incredibly demanding. You can't have all the answers or skills you'll need before you begin. You need friends who will pick you up when you're down, challenge you when you're being ridiculous, and give you a kick when you're being lazy.

## Bishop John Went

Meeting regularly to reflect and review with an experienced mentor will be hugely valuable. A possible alternative (or addition) to this would be joining a reflective-practice group with others involved in pioneer ministry.

## Chris Howson

Help your fresh expression to genuinely reflect the needs of the context, and to be shaped by those who get involved. There will need to be a real sense of ownership by as many people as possible. I also believe that we can allow fresh expressions of Church to change and to die. In a fast-flowing inner-city context, communities may change rapidly and projects might ebb and flow. What is important is whether, during their life, each pioneering initiative is a channel for the work of the Holy Spirit in the communities and individuals involved.

## Chris Neal

It is important to recognize that the work has to be shaped by the mind and heart of Christ. When taking God's people to a new place, there must be an understanding that this may well be a lonely, long and misunderstood process. There will be many set-backs and even opposition, much of which may come from other expressions of Christian community. It is at this point that the pioneer and his or her community need to remember Philippians 3.10 – that they might know every day the presence of the risen Jesus, in order that they might have the courage to share in his servanthood and sufferings, become like him in his dying, believing in the ultimate promise and vindication of the resurrection.

## Dan Pierce

Take it day by day and keep praying.

## Ellen Louden

I would emphasize good pastoral care, good communication networks, a clear strategy for developing worship and groups in which relationships can flourish, a clear focus on mission and service that is shared by the whole community and, lastly, making sure it stays fun and edifying for those involved.

## Ian Bell

Keep Jesus at the centre of everything and concentrate on forming life-long, whole-life, disciple-making followers of Jesus.

## Ian Meredith

Seek advice. Don't be scared. Talk about everything all the time so that everyone knows where they are on the journey. The community is not just about the leader's decisions. Make sure ideas about growth are communicated well in advance and are an integral part of the DNA from the start.

## Janet Webb

I would underline the need for prayer, pastoral support and help with strategic planning. Pioneering can be an isolating experience, so the trinity of prayer, pastoral support and strategic thinking alongside others are key to keeping a pioneer sane.

## Jo Cox

Build a good team and have interests outside of the fresh expression.

## Joe Knight

I love Dietrich Bonhoeffer's challenge in *Life Together*, where he states that those who love their dream of community will end up 'being the destroyer' of community. But he goes on to say that if you love those around you, then community will be created. I think this is a great place to start a fresh expression and a great help when thinking about sustaining it. Loving those around us, even when they cause hurt, discomfort and disunity, will sustain any community. Loving others will help the fresh expression stay fresh, because it will be able to see, adapt and serve peoples needs in and out of season. The definition of love that is found embodied in Jesus blesses, challenges, welcomes, disciplines, heals and restores. It is to this love that all fresh expressions of church invite others, and it is in this love that all fresh expressions will find and sustain life over a long period of time.

## John Drane

Don't expect miracles as of right, but don't be surprised when they happen.

## Jonny Baker

Can *you* sustain you? That is, are you in this for the long haul in terms of discipleship? Prophets get a hard time. Pioneers have adventure and excitement, but there's struggle and heartache and not a lot of money! Make sure your expectations are right because people get disillusioned when there was an illusion. To do that you will need friends for the journey. If you're not sure where to look, connect with a mission community like CMS. I was very interested in Beth Keith's research for Fresh Expressions on pioneers. It demonstrated that pioneers who connected into sodalities like CMS or Church Army were finding the journey a lot better! Then secondly think upfront about issues of financial sustainability. What sort of model of community and funding are you imagining? There are a lot of projects with hefty funding for three years who then find it hard to keep going when the money is all gone.

## Mark Berry

Pioneers should ask themselves how they might continue to be a pioneer in community. I think we need to move away from the expectation that pioneers have to always-and-only start new communities, and that the pioneering stage is a formative one. We need pioneers and prophets in all our churches and communities. They will challenge stagnation, read the signs of the times and lead by living as pioneers. Pioneers need support rather than yes-men, and critical friends rather than conflict! Pioneers need accountability but not to be controlled or judged by the measures of old. As a pioneer I have no desire to create something that becomes institutional or static – therefore we need to find new ways of talking about sustainability and evaluation. For example, how are we sustaining the creative heart of the community? How are we sharing and living our vision? How are we being peacemakers? I think we need to challenge the language and practice of community. Rather than simply asking where the money is coming from, I suggest we have to ask how we can live more simply. Rather than finding ways to look more like the institution, we need to be living differently. Rather than measuring 'success' we need to share stories of lives and communities being changed. I am aware that this is difficult, and in the current financial mess it raises huge challenges, but I think we need to struggle with this even if it means we cannot live or minister in the way the Church has always expected. Faith is a big thing and I am becoming more and more convinced that we are heading to a simpler way of living as church communities that is far more orientated around faithfulness and simplicity – less *professional* and more sacramental. We are not there yet and we do need money and we need to honour those who support us and seek to be creative both in terms of spiritual capital and financial capital. But in the long term I see fewer and fewer fully paid ministers (including pioneers) and more and more community exercised ministries. For those of us used to being paid, including myself, it is going to be hard going.

## Robert Warren

Take Sabbath seriously and nurture people's ability to relax, play, be creative and not take themselves too seriously.

## Steve Clarke

In the community in which I am involved we are trying to connect creatively with the wider local Christian family. In our context this looks like a more established relationship with the cathedral in Gloucester. We are also adapting an idea from Home in Oxford – looking at how we can maintain a rhythm of life that sustains and releases people.

## Steve Hollinghurst

It is important to ensure that whatever emerges will be ultimately led by those who have come to faith as part of its witness. They need to be allowed to shape how it is run and how it worships.

## Further reading

Adams, I., *Cave, Refectory, Road: Monastic Rhythms for Contemporary Living*, Norwich: Canterbury Press, 2010.

Barry, P. (OSB) (translation), *Saint Benedict's Rule*, Mahwah: Hidden Spring, 2004.

Bonhoeffer, D., *Life Together*, London: SCM Press, 1954.

Bradley, I., *Colonies of Heaven: Celtic Models for Today's Church*, London: Darton, Longman & Todd, 2000.

Cray, G., Mobsby, I. and Kennedy, A. (eds), *Ancient Faith, Future Mission: New Monasticism as Fresh Expression of Church*, Norwich: Canterbury Press, 2010.

Croft, S. and Mobsby, I. (eds), *Ancient Faith, Future Mission: Fresh Expressions in the Sacramental Tradition*, Norwich: Canterbury Press, 2009.

Hirst, J., *Struggling to be Holy*, London: Darton, Longman & Todd, 2006.

Jamison, C., *Finding Sanctuary: Monastic Steps for Everyday Life*, London: Phoenix, 2007.

Lawrence, J., *Growing Leaders: Reflections on Leadership, Life and Jesus*, Oxford: Bible Reading Fellowship, 2004.

Moynagh, M. and Freeman, A., Share Booklets 01–07, Warwick: Fresh Expressions, 2011.

Myers, J. R., *Organic Community: Creating a Place Where People Naturally Connect*, Grand Rapids: Baker Books, 2007.

Rutba House, *Schools for Conversion: 12 Marks of a New Monasticism*, Eugene: Cascade Books, 2005.

Sheffield Centre, 'Northumbria Community: Matching Monastery and Mission', *Encounters on the Edge* 29, 2006.

Vanier, J., *Community and Growth*, London: Darton, Longman & Todd, 2007.

Williams, R., *Silence and Honey Cakes: The Wisdom of the Desert*, Oxford: Lion Hudson, 2004.

Wilson-Hartgrove, J., *New Monasticism: What it has to say to Today's Church*, Grand Rapids: Brazos Press, 2008.

## Members of the Research Group

**Jonny Baker** directs the Pioneer Mission Leadership Training for the Church Mission Society. He is author of *Alternative Worship* and *Curating Worship*.

**Ian Bell** is the coordinator of VentureFX for the Methodist Church.

**Mark Berry** is the Pioneer Leader of Safespace – a new monastic community in Telford. Mark teaches at the Centre for Youth Ministry and the CMS Pioneer Ministry Course.

**Mark Bryant** is the Bishop of Jarrow.

**Steve Clarke** is a pioneer minister in Gloucester and curate at Gloucester Cathedral.

**Jo Cox** is the Evangelism in Contemporary Culture Officer for the Methodist Church. She is co-editor of *The Call and the Commission*.

**John Drane** is a best-selling author, affiliate professor of New Testament and Practical Theology at the Brehm Center for Worship Theology and the Arts at Fuller Seminary, and deputy chair of the board of the Mission-Shaped Ministry course.

**Ben Edson** is Diocesan Fresh Expressions Missioner for the Manchester Diocese, Team Vicar and Missioner at St James and Emmanuel, Didsbury and an Associate Missioner with fresh expressions. Ben pioneered Sanctus1, a Fresh Expression of Church, in Manchester city centre and was involved in establishing Nexus Art Cafe.

**Steve Hollinghurst** is Researcher in Evangelism to Post-Christian Culture at the Church Army Sheffield Centre – a mission think tank and research unit. He is the author of *Mission Shaped Evangelism*.

**Chris Howson** is the City Centre Mission Priest for the City of Bradford and is linked to two fresh expressions of Church in the city. He is the author of *A Just Church*.

**Beth Keith** works for Church Army's Sheffield Centre, researching fresh expressions of Church and developing learning networks of pioneers and evangelists with the fresh expressions team.

**Joe Knight** and his wife Kim are in the process of establishing a house of prayer in an old vicarage in Gloucester.

**Stephen Lindridge** is a Methodist presbyter and the National Methodist Missioner for Fresh Expressions.

**Ellen Loudon** is a parish priest in the diocese of Liverpool. Alongside her parish ministry she is currently developing RiverArts, a network for Christian artists and creative people.

**Ned Lunn** is an ordinand at Cranmer Hall, Durham, and has a background in theatre direction.

**Ian Meredith** runs his own business and describes himself as a dad, a husband, a disciple of Jesus, a friend, a student, a thinker, a missionary and a coffee drinker.

**Chris Neal** is Director of Mission for the Church Mission Society (CMS). Prior to this he was Rector of the Thame Valley Team Ministry – during which time he planted five congregations and 40 new cell groups.

**Ben Norton** is pioneer minister based in Bridlington East Yorkshire. He has pioneered two fresh expressions of church – including XY lads' church, which is featured on a Fresh Expressions DVD. He is the author of *Espresso Scriptures*.

**Dan Pierce** is a pioneer ordinand studying for an MA at Cranmer Hall, Durham.

**Janet Sutton Webb** is the United Reformed Church's first full-time pioneer minister. After six years in traditional church ministry she moved to the South West and is currently experimenting in forming emerging Christian communities.

**Sue Wallace** ran the Visions alternative worship community for 18 years and is now the Team Vicar for Leeds Parish Church. She is the author of *Multi-Sensory Prayer*.

**Robert Warren** is a former vicar of St Thomas', Crookes, Sheffield. He was the Church of England's National Officer for Evangelism and a Springboard Missioner. He is one of the authors of *Emmaus* and has written a number of other books. He is recently retired.

**John Went** is the Bishop of Tewkesbury.

**David Wilkinson** is the Principal of St John's College, Durham and the author of a number of significant books. He regularly contributes to *Thought for the Day* on BBC Radio 4.

# Conclusion
# Fresh: A Call to be Apostolic, Catholic, Holy and One

The Nicene Creed describes the true Church as having four qualities. It should be:

- One.
- Holy.
- Catholic (meaning 'universal', rather than 'Roman Catholic').
- Apostolic.

For many centuries Christians have seen these 'four marks of the Church' as both rooted in scripture and a sure guide for the Church of the future. As the authors of this book we entirely concur – and hope that all fresh expressions and pioneer ministries exhibit those qualities.

But it would be disingenuous to suggest that, in terms of Church, fresh expressions and pioneer ministry are merely 'more of the same'. In many respects they turn assumptions about traditional Church upside-down. They often meet outside of a recognized church building, they use forms of worship often very different from traditional forms of worship and they are led by people who often look very different from traditional ministers – of any denomination. Being turned upside-down is disorientating, but it can sometimes be part of the purposes of God.

We suggest that fresh expressions and pioneer ministry do seek to embody the same four marks of the Church – but in reverse order. Thus fresh expressions are:

- Apostolic.
- Catholic.
- Holy.
- One.

Hitherto, while the four marks have been notionally equal, some have been more equal than others. In particular the last, 'apostolic', has either been marginalized or seen in terms of the 'apostolic succession'. The debate as to who does – and does not – succeed from the first apostles has its value, but also has more than a whiff of ecclesiastical one-upmanship; it all too easily descends into a debate about who gets to wear the theological trousers. But apostolic has a different and arguably richer meaning than this.

## Apostolic

We argue that the primary meaning of apostolic concerns mission. The word, as we have noted several times, means 'sent'. A Church that is apostolic is a Church being *sent* on the mission of God. An apostolic Church is a Church that spreads the good news in word and deed. The sin it continually confesses is the sin of insularity, whereby Jesus is seen as a possession to be enjoyed not a treasure to be shared. The form of Church an apostolic Church always shuns is the Church as in-crowd or club. The member of the Trinity an apostolic Church is especially careful to honour is God the Holy Spirit – that person of the Trinity whom the Western Church – Catholic *and* Protestant – has most tended to sideline. Apostolic churches honour the Spirit because he is par excellence the divine fuel for mission, without whom we can do nothing. Churches that sideline the Spirit are inherently unmissional.

As we pray that the Church might become more apostolic in the next 20 years, such prayers include the following. We pray:

- that the churches will start a lot more churches – given past experience, it looks as if God likes plenty of them

- that each bishop, District Chair or Synod Moderator plant one church per year
- that experience of being a church-planter becomes recognized as a fundamental prerequisite of anyone engaged in episcopal/ oversight ministry
- that the Church in Britain will grow substantially in numbers
- that it will grow substantially in those areas where it is currently weak and among those communities where it is currently ignored.

If this seems impossible, then think of the church in China over the last decades. In 1949, with the Chinese Communist revolution, Christianity in China looked doomed. Largely the import of Western missionaries, who were then kicked out by the Communists, it was seen as foreign, capitalist, a relic of colonialism and the opium of the people. After 1949, Christians and churches experienced ruthless persecution for decades. Notwithstanding such treatment, the Chinese churches grew, most especially those informal, unregulated forms of Church. Some 60 years on, China may well become the world's largest Christian nation during the present century – reflecting the apostolic quality of Chinese Christians.

*As you come to the end of this book, how is God challenging you to be apostolic in your Christian life?*

## Catholic

Being catholic means a recognition of the vast breadth of the Church. Often breadth in church-speak means anything goes. This reduces breadth to a version of that cultural niceness of the English where being good means appearing politely to agree and ignoring difference. But this is not catholicity, it is hypocrisy.

The Christian Church is broad, but in a different way. It is broad across time – 20 centuries of time. So being catholic means a respect for, a love of, the vast heritage we have as Christians.

One of the delightful aspects of fresh expressions is where they have grasped some nugget of the Christian tradition and recalibrated it for the present – such as the Celtic saints or monasticism. Of course, respect for the past requires a readiness to hear it as it is, not to remake it in our own image; to hear, for instance, the fierce rigour of the Celtic Church, not some soft-focus confection with pan-pipe accompaniment.

The Christian Church is broad by stretching around the globe. So being catholic means a respect for, a love of, the vast Christian family of which we are a part. This is hugely encouraging, for while many Western churches have struggled, many churches worldwide are growing. Already the Church in Britain is being re-formed by Christians of different ethnicities, and this will only increase in the future.

The Christian Church is broad because of the huge range of different churches. So being catholic means a respect for, a love of, the range of different ways of following Jesus. We do disagree, sometimes on very serious matters. But being catholic means looking first, not at what we dislike about another Church or Christian, but at what we can learn from another Christian or another church.

As we pray that the Church might become more catholic in the next 20 years, we pray:

- that we celebrate what was good in the Church of the past, treating generations before us not as fuddy-duddies to be looked down upon, but pioneers from whom we can learn
- for a humility before Christians and churches from other lands and a readiness to learn from them, though also for an unromantic recognition of their imperfections
- for a humility in local churches, recognizing that we are only complete in relationship to our sister churches
- for a 'godly plagiarism' that gladly borrows from the good things in other traditions, old and new, British and overseas, from our own denomination and from others
- for the diversification of our fellowships, especially in terms of ethnicity, making churches genuinely multiracial places

- for a humility from the so-called 'mainline' denominations towards churches rooted in different ethnicities and new churches, whom we have often ignored or even looked down upon – and which have much to teach us.

*From which parts of the Church catholic could you learn?*

## Holy

Being holy is, above all, that mark of the Church that is not ours to achieve but ours to receive. Holiness comes only through the grace of God. But we can block it or nurture it. We can think differently about holiness in terms of what we focus on about it. The word most often paired with 'holy' is 'trinity'. Despite being notionally Trinitarian, Christian churches often operate practically as bi-nitarian or even unitarian, focusing on one or two persons, not on all three. And in the West, the two persons who tend to be emphasized are the Father and the Son. Holiness could therefore start with a fresh seeing of God as Trinity, who is so revealed in the scriptures, across the Christian tradition and pre-eminently in the life of Jesus.

Since, as we argued in Chapter 1, the God of the Holy Trinity is a pioneering God, a God whose life is mission, in whom Jesus is mission incarnate, this would indicate that mission is the heart of holiness. That is to say that when we imagine that holiness is, say, 'love' or 'purity' or 'endurance', these are not abstract nouns but qualities *for* something. Holy love is love *for* God, *for* others. And since God's mission is specific and urgent, holy love is for now and for the people with whom we share our lives, our street, our town.

As we pray that the Church might become more holy in the next 20 years, we pray for:

- heartfelt repentance of our unholiness and a turning back to receive the triune God through Jesus

- renewed commitment to being salt and light in society, while lamenting the unholiness of society
- a fresh openness to God as the Holy Trinity, the doctrinal engine-room of the Christian faith – and repentance of un-Trinitarian ways of thinking, being and acting
- a fresh seeking of the Holy Spirit, God unbound, with a readiness to receive the unpredictable consequences of letting the Spirit work in us
- a fresh ambition for our individual and corporate discipleship, to become fully 'mature in Christ', fuelled by the recognition that, whether we believe in ourselves, the incarnation of Jesus proves that God believes in us.

*In what ways do you need to repent of an unambitious discipleship?*

## One

All too often Christians have seen being 'one' in terms of being one in doctrine, structure and liturgy. Unity has therefore been the unity of doctrinal statements, ecclesiastical structures and liturgical uniformity. But since God is beyond the words we have to describe him, it is not surprising that within the Christian tradition we have a godly variety of ways of naming him. Moreover, given the sinfulness of human beings, it is not entirely surprising that we find it hard to agree. Seeking closer agreement on doctrine, structure and liturgy has virtues, but the experience of the last century suggests that we should not hold our breath in the hope of some great reunification of the churches. Besides, would a single, global 'McChurch' be such a great thing anyway? Instead, Christians could enjoy such common ground as we have (and there is a lot of it), and focus on the mission of God and the way Christians can unite in prayer.

The great thing about seeking oneness around mission is that there is broad recognition that the mission of God is huge and multifaceted. The scriptures, tradition and the contemporary churches show that it is word and deed, evangelism and social action, kingdom and Church, fresh expression and traditional parish – and much more besides. Moreover there is wide agreement that God has created human beings with a great array of gifts in a wide range of contexts. Thus we can enjoy the fact that some churches and Christians do mission more as evangelism and others more in terms of social action, since there is value in all such work and since none is on its own sufficient. The task is huge – so we could express our oneness in the unity of our application to the task of mission and be less neurotic about everyone doing everything the same. Instead of asking whether fresh expressions and pioneer ministry are better, or whether traditional parishes are superior, we might simply grow up into the mission to which God is calling us.

And while Christians struggle to get complete agreement about doctrine and structure, there is much broader agreement about prayer. We all, in theory, think it is a good idea. Christians of all strands have found it possible to unite in prayer, so we could see 'oneness' in terms of *doing* prayer.

As we pray that the Church might become more one in the next 20 years, we pray:

- that Christians learn to pray together for this country – perhaps the Week of Prayer for Christian Unity could be renamed the Week of Prayer for the Nation?
- that Christians learn to support each other's mission
- that Christians root our oneness in mission and prayer rather than in doctrine, structures and liturgy – and let that unity percolate into doctrine, structures and liturgy

This has significant implications for ecumenism as a whole. Too often ecumenism is lived out as a rather flabby desire to be nice rather than a zeal for the mission of God. The ecumenical movement's unofficial motto has tended, in the words of Bob Marley, to be 'let's get together and feel alright'. But it could have a different, more eschatological, motto – the words of a leader who saw the future thus:

I've seen the Promised Land. I may not get there with you. But I want you to know tonight, that we, as a people, will get to the Promised Land. So I'm happy, tonight. I'm not worried about anything. I'm not fearing any man. Mine eyes have seen the glory of the coming of the Lord.

Martin Luther King, Jr

We've listed a lot of prayers in the last few pages. It's time to stop writing and start praying! God often uses each of us to be part of the answer to the prayers we make. This is a sobering and intoxicating challenge.

*If your heart echoes some of the prayers we have mentioned, might that be God's call to you, that you should be part of answering of those some prayers?*

Jesus said to them again, 'Peace be with you. As the Father has sent me, so I send you.' When he had said this, he breathed on them and said to them, 'Receive the Holy Spirit.' (John 20.21–2)

# Index